GROW YOUR CHURCH!

OVERCOME THE BIGGEST OBSTACLE TO CHURCH GROWTH AND GET 85% OF YOUR FIRST-TIME VISITORS TO RETURN

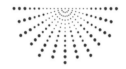

REV. TRACY BARNOWE

APOCRYPHILE
PRESS

Apocryphile Press
1700 Shattuck Ave #81
Berkeley, CA 94709
www.apocryphilepress.com

Copyright © 2018 by Tracy Barnowe
Printed in the United States of America
ASIN 000000000 | kindle
ISBN 978-1-949643-00-8 | paperback
ISBN 978-1-949643-01-5 | epub

Please join our mailing list at
www.apocryphilepress.com/free
We'll keep you up-to-date on all our new releases,
and we'll also send you a FREE BOOK.
Visit us today!

CONTENTS

To GadtheHero, without whom
this book would never have existed.
In situations requiring a hero,
he always knows just exactly what to say.

INTRODUCTION

I was raised in the Episcopal Church and was fully involved. My family attended church every Sunday. I was in Sunday school and then youth group and youth choir. When I was big enough to carry the heavy wooden torches and eventually the inlaid stained-glass cross, I served as an acolyte. I was trained as a lector at Grace Cathedral. I was baptized and confirmed in the Episcopal Church. So when I moved to another state to go to college, it felt natural to seek out my local Episcopal church and start attending.

I worked four jobs putting myself through college and carried a full academic load. For one of my jobs, I often worked on a setup crew for a popular event space on campus. This meant that free time and the extra sleep I could have had on Sunday morning were rare luxuries. It also meant that I was often working late on Saturday nights, so getting up Sunday mornings was especially difficult. I didn't have a car and the bus service on Sundays was reduced, so I had to walk 1.3 miles each way to get to church and I often did it in pumps because I had been raised to dress your best for church. The room that I rented was on the far edge of frat row, so I had to walk through several blocks of frat houses on the morning after their biggest parties.

One Sunday I walked past a house with an enormous front lawn that was edged by a cement ledge about a foot higher than the sidewalk. The grass was strewn with empty beer cans; nearly every square foot had one and many had spilled down onto the sidewalk and were littering my path. As I walked past the house, one of the cans in front of me lurched slightly. I froze. It lurched again, this time skittering a few inches across the cement with a hollow plinking sound before skidding to a halt. My eyes widened and my stomach grew queasy as I wondered what kind of critter might have gotten itself trapped in there. The can teetered there for a few seconds, then suddenly began to pick up speed, smacked into the ledge and then with a sickening jerk careened up and over the cement wall and leapt up onto the lawn, heading toward the house with a strange and unnatural motion.

It was then that I saw the fishing line glinting in the sun. I followed it with my eyes to find two fraternity brothers in sunglasses staring at me intently. They were sitting in their boxer shorts on a pair of lawn chairs on the roof overhanging the wrap-around porch. A fishing pole was in their hands, and they watched with inebriated concentration to see if I would follow the can. I shook my head with uneasy laughter and exasperation, waved to them, and continued down the sidewalk, kicking the beer cans out of my way as I went. This was not the first or the last uncomfortable scene I would have to walk through to get to this church.

Each Sunday after service, I made a point of going through the receiving line at the back of the sanctuary. I shook the minister's hand and told him how much I enjoyed the sermon. I hung out during coffee hour and diligently said hello to folks I had seen in the coffee hour the previous week.

I did this every Sunday for three months.

After three months, one Sunday during the coffee hour, the minister approached me and shook my hand. He said, "Hello there, is this your first Sunday visiting with us?"

I never went back.

Five years later I found myself in Portland, Oregon. My fiancé and I were moving into a new apartment in anticipation of our wedding the following month. One of the long-term tenants, a 93-year-old woman named Mollie, came out to stand on her front step and watch the goings-on. And for the first time in decades, she locked herself out. I crawled in her bedroom window, clambering in my hiking boots, shorts and sweaty tank-top over the doilies and tiny porcelain bric-a-brac on her dresser so that I could open the front door to let her in. After that we were fast friends. Soon after I asked her if she knew much about the church two doors up the street, a small congregational church from a denomination I had never heard of—the United Church of Christ. She said she attended, so I asked if I could go with her some time. The next Sunday we walked together across the small alley to the church.

In heels, Mollie was half my height with a generous measuring stick. She slipped her arm through mine and took me around and introduced me to every single person in the church that day. I met 50 people, most of them more than three times my age. I made a point of signing the guest book. Two days later I received a lovely letter from the interim minister congratulating me on my upcoming wedding, welcoming me to the area, and telling me how much he enjoyed meeting me. The following week I went back to church and—as people often do—everyone had changed their outfits. I only remembered Mollie's name and maybe one other person. Yet every single person came up, shook my hand, called me by name and told me how glad they were to see me.

I joined that church the following year. Fourteen years later I was ordained in that same sanctuary.

I write this book as a gift to all of the progressive churches that are in decline. To all the churches that are wondering why people come to visit pretty regularly but never come back. To all the churches with rich histories of doing critical work in their communities, but whose leadership is now older and grayer and wondering how much longer they can keep these vital ministries going. Your story doesn't have to end.

I've worked with a lot of churches and listened to their stories, their worries, and their theories on what has caused their decline and the national decline. Here is what I know:

First, we have suffered enormous blows in the public eye due to scandals in mainline conservative denominations and the Catholic Church. It is easy to cast the blame on guilty-by-association scapegoating, but the reality is that the Christian Church Universal has an integrity problem both within its doors and in the public eye, and whether we were actively involved or not, it is our mess to clean up, our reputation to rebuild, our wound to heal.

Second, we have lost valuable skills in the areas of evangelism and welcoming newcomers. I hesitate even to say the word evangelism because for progressives it conjures up images of people standing on street corners with megaphones and large signs with lists of those whom God hates. It conjures up images of rich televangelists promising healing of terminal illnesses through the television waves if people only send checks. It conjures up images of men and women in starched suits standing on your doorstep handing you copies of the Watchtower. So we run from talking about our faith. We live divided lives and learn to keep our Sunday activities to ourselves the rest of the week. We pointedly ignore the visitors in our church for fear of alienating them or pressuring them, and pat ourselves on the back for not being like "those bible-thumpers." As a result, I use the words "interpersonal outreach" to describe outreach that is focused on inviting our friends and acquaintances to church.

Third, we have become discouraged, overwhelmed, and paralyzed. We have watched as our churches split over social justice issues and infighting. We have watched as the children all grew up and left. We have watched as our congregations have grown older and grayer, with fewer and fewer people able to keep up with all the church used to do. We argue among ourselves about what would make a difference, and bat around angry missives about the music, the budget, the preaching, the website, the fliers, how nobody volunteers to help anymore, and how we're about ready to quit out of frustration. We spend enormous amounts of money on consultants to assess our vitality and tell us whether or not we should just close our doors. We read books on "redefining church" and wonder whether starting an expensive Wednesday night Taizé service in the local sports bar might just give us that fresh new look all the Millennials are wanting.

Meanwhile, in most of the churches that I talk with, a steady stream of one-to-two visitors per week silently come in and then leave again, never to return.

I write this book because most of the churches that I have worked with don't realize that there are simple solutions to all of these problems. Integrity can be rebuilt. We can welcome the stranger and sojourner, and make disciples of all nations, without being offensive, aggressive, or pernicious. We can relearn skills that will make enormous headway in jolting us out of our paralysis, and we can rebuild our optimism, momentum, and sense of God's vision for our churches. These skills cost nothing to apply and can make an enormous difference in our church's vitality.

If you have a steady stream of visitors—no matter how small— and if you are willing to learn new skills, your church is viable. I wrote this book like I designed my workshops—to give you practical information that can be immediately applied for measurable results.

Many blessings,

Rev. Tracy Barnowe
Culver City, California
August, 2018

IT'S ALL A MATTER OF MINDSET AND SKILL SET

*Y*ou should know that I almost didn't become a minister, and that I almost didn't go into church growth. I have been going to church since I was a child. I felt the call to ministry in 2005 and enrolled in seminary full of excitement. I took classes part-time for more than a year and found all the material really interesting. I loved learning about the Bible. I loved learning about theology. I found biblical history to be fascinating.

In 2008 I moved to Berkeley and pursued my Master of Divinity full-time. At this point, I had to take Field Education for a year. I began working fifteen hours a week at a lovely local church. I basically followed the minister around and did everything she did. I preached once a month, and I kind of enjoyed that, but that was about all I enjoyed. Don't get me wrong, the people were all lovely. It was the work that didn't quite fit. I helped plan a couple of funerals, which I found tedious, mostly because I didn't know the deceased or their families at all. I didn't like choosing the music for Sunday worship, so I always waited until the last minute and then tried to get the church secretary to just do it for me. I got hauled into a come-to-Jesus meeting with the Field

Education department when the secretary eventually ratted me out.

I observed the Bible study class, which was a slog. The same members had been coming forever and they had been working their way through the Book of Acts for three years. I went to council meetings where people argued with the minister about attendance. I didn't understand the stress levels when some simple changes—it seemed to me—could make all the difference. I went to worship-planning meetings, which always seemed to take longer than they needed to. The most fun I had was when I went to ladies' crafting/church bazaar meetings, because the ladies were a hoot and at least I could take my knitting—but I didn't really feel like I was being a minister. I went to weekly meetings with the minister. I went to mission board meetings. I went to meetings and more meetings...

I tried to help with serving communion twice. The first time, the minister got a perpetual nosebleed—I mean it just plain wouldn't stop for the duration of the worship service. She made me elevate the elements so she wouldn't get blood all over them while she spoke the words of blessing. Her head was tipped back so that her chin jutted fiercely at the congregation. Blood was quickly soaking the wad of tissues she had stuffed into her nostrils. I seriously questioned the wisdom of both of us wearing white robes that day. She pinched her nose with one hand while she dabbed at it ferociously with the other. I stared fixedly at the congregation and pretended not to be seriously disturbed by the wads of tissues speckled bright red pumping furiously up and down to my right. "...and Desus said...Twacy, pweez ewebate da host...*sniff*...dis is my body, bwoken fo you...*dab*..." I stood paralyzed in front of the congregation with the bread in my hands, going through the motions until finally, finally, an eternity later, communion was over and she allowed herself to be taken by the ushers back to her office during the final hymn. The second the door closed behind her, we breathed a collective sigh of relief.

"This is my nose," I thought, "broken for you. This is my blood, sneezed out for you." I didn't know whether to laugh or cry.

The second time, it was All Saints' Sunday. There was an elaborate and sprawling display in front of the altar. Creative and artistic church mice had draped shimmering lamé in shades of blue over multiple connected tables cluttered with cake plates and boxes to create the semblance of a frothing river flowing over uneven rocks and logs. Numerous bowls of sand were placed hither and thither. With great solemnity all 200 congregants came up to light toothpick-thin 12-inch taper candles on one end, and then reverently place them—one for each saint they had lost—into a bowl of sand. People came up and lit candle after candle. People filled the aisles. The whole display sparkled with hundreds of flames reflected by the shimmering lamé. Eventually, the last person sat down. I stood next to the minister in my robe and as the music died she began the words for the Holy Eucharist.

All of a sudden two men at the back of the sanctuary leapt up and ran out to the side-aisles, one on each side. With the fury of Olympic sprinters they pounded down toward the front of the sanctuary, arms pumping. My first thought was to wonder which deceased but not-so-forgiving loved one they had dared to forget to light a candle for. At the front of the sanctuary they made hard 90-degree turns, heading right for the display, coming at it—and each other—from both sides. They lunged toward the center of the display so fast that they accidentally cracked their heads together and you could hear the sharp snap of bone on bone echo through the sanctuary. They reeled backward in pain, holding their foreheads with one hand and blinking back tears while they commenced to slap and smash at the display with their bare hands, knocking bowls to the floor, snapping dozens of candles in half with each blow, and sending sand flying in all directions. The congregation stared, paralyzed, and clung to each other.

Apparently, someone had lit and then placed one single ultra-thin taper into the sand at a bit of an angle and perhaps not quite deep enough to hold it steady. It had been slowly, ever-so-slowly, tipping toward the lamé—which is incredibly flammable. Unbeknownst to anyone—even to themselves—we just so happened to have two different fire chiefs from two different counties in our sanctuary that day. They had sat on opposite sides of the sanctuary and had been watching the entire display—and that particular taper—like hawks. The second it touched the lamé, they leapt into action.

In the end, I was standing behind the altar with my mouth open while acrid greenish-black smoke billowed four feet deep along the ceiling. I beheld a scene of hundreds of broken and extinguished candles littering the carpet. Charred fabric with a gaping and blackened four-foot hole burnt in it was strewn across the tables and floor in front of the altar. Sand was everywhere. Two large men with blackened hands and sooty faces held their foreheads, gasping for breath and grimacing in pain as the congregation stared in wide-eyed, confused horror.

This was only my second attempt to serve communion. I started thinking that perhaps God was giving me a sign of biblical proportions.

After what seemed to be a crystal clear call to ministry and almost two years of seminary, I was at the point where I was convinced it just wasn't my gig. It was boring (except for the occasional communion disaster; those really got the blood pumping). It felt tedious, monotonous. It was definitely not what I thought it was going to be. And also, I just wasn't very good at it. I wasn't patient. I wasn't good at going with the flow. If I saw a problem and saw a solution, I wasn't good at patiently waiting through months of committee meetings to slowly convince people to give me permission to just solve the problem. I didn't like volunteering to do something single-handedly and being politely ignored. I didn't like sitting through meetings just so we could fulfill our every-third-Tuesday requirement in the by-laws. I was not good at politicking.

I began pursuing simultaneously a Master's Degree in Biblical Studies to hedge my bets, so the course credits I had accumulated wouldn't go to waste. I figured that with an MA at least I could teach at community college. At that point I seriously didn't think the ministry thing was going to work out. When I was done with my year of Field Education, both the minister and I agreed that I sounded more passionate when I talked about my thesis on the Old Testament than I ever sounded when I talked about what I was doing at her church. She wished me well and I dug into Ancient Hebrew.

Around that time I was invited to a seminarians' conference at the national headquarters of the United Church of Christ in Cleveland, Ohio. A few weeks before the conference, I got an email from the denomination about a Gallup assessment for people interested in *church planting* and *church revitalization*. I had never heard of either of those terms. On a whim I took the assessment, and a few days later I got a call from the denomination. Apparently I had scored pretty high—they said I had the highest score in the history of the test. They started asking me about my background and asked me to send in a resume. This made no sense to me, because nothing I had done before was anything close to ministry. I sent them my professional resume, which was mostly administrative/office management roles. I sent them my volunteer resume, which had some things I had done both inside of and outside of churches.

I remember getting a phone call that changed my life. "You've planted five organizations and revitalized at least seven. How come we've never heard of you?!" I'd never really thought of it like that before. Sure, I'd invented a couple of things and started a couple of businesses, groups, and organizations. I had volunteered for a few stagnating groups over the years that had really great visions but no real oomph. I had helped get them going. I had seen some community issues here and there and organized some folks to deal with them. It was something I always seemed to be doing in my spare time. It was fun.

But I never thought of doing that with or for churches. This may sound naïve, but until that moment it had simply never occurred to me that effective outreach, first-time visitor retention, launching programs, organizing people to address social justice issues in the community, and proven growth strategies might be something churches needed.

I was baffled and intrigued at the same time.

I went to the conference and signed up for all the workshops on planting, revitalization, and church growth. On the one hand the data—and especially case studies—was fascinating. On the other hand, just about all of the methods they were discussing were things I had already used successfully with other organizations. I had a brief post-assessment interview with a couple of the denominational staff in outreach. I remember being really surprised when they said I should be teaching this stuff rather than learning it, because I had so much experience.

I was shocked to learn how many churches were declining across the nation. None of the classes in seminary had ever mentioned any of this. I was blown away by the whole experience. I left that conference filled not only with a stronger call to ministry, but with the distinct feeling that for the first time in my life I was in the right place at the right time with the right set of skills.

I also left with a distinct understanding and belief that has never left me since: *Church growth is about mindset and skill set. Anyone can do it if they are willing to learn. One does not have to be an ordained minister or a "growth specialist" to become good at it.*

A few months later, I attended a church that happened to be looking for a Sunday school teacher. They asked me to meet with them about it, and I declined the position. They were adamant they wanted to hire me. I asked why, and they thought someone like me might bring in more families with children. So we started talking about what they were doing and why they weren't getting the results they wanted. We talked for over two hours and I helped them understand why their efforts weren't effective and I helped them develop a better plan for growth.

In the end, they hired me as Director of Family and Spiritual Ministries for ten hours a week, and within three months I more than doubled their Sunday school attendance. We changed the focus of Sunday school and started doing more social justice-focused activities. Their kids started inviting their friends. The older folks started inviting their friends. A local school called and asked if we could lead an assembly about what caused poverty, what our Sunday school was doing about it, and what they could do to get involved. We discovered that the kids were talking to their friends and teachers about what they were doing in church every week. Since then, I have used the same methods at three different churches with similar results.

The data is clear. If you are reading this, you are in the right place at the right time. I can teach you what you need to know. God will take care of the rest. If you are willing to learn some basic skills and trust God, you can turn your church from declining to thriving.

In 2009, I started with one piece of hard data about return rates I learned at that seminarians' conference and then tested it in multiple churches. I wanted to see if it was true (it was), and then I wanted to beat it. I developed and refined a method for follow-up with first-time visitors and tracked the numbers over the next six years. I was able to consistently get 88% of first-time visitors to return the following Sunday, with at least 50% of them staying to get actively involved and attend regularly for the long-term. I turned this knowledge into a workshop, so it has been tested in numerous churches with similar results. Eventually I got tired of traveling every weekend to teach, so I turned the workshop into this book.

This book is ideal for churches that get a steady stream of one to two visitors each week who just never come back. This book will walk you through everything you need to do, step by step, with practical instructions, scripts, and clear tips to avoid common pitfalls. It teaches you how to do it right, no matter what role you play in the church. It will work for ushers, greeters, welcome teams, ministers, or anyone who sits in the pews every Sunday. I promise that if you learn this method on a Saturday, you can use it successfully on Sunday.

2

WHY THE CHURCH IS NOT
DECLINING, AND WHY IT IS

*E*verybody has an opinion for why churches are declining these days. The sexual abuse scandals of the Catholic church decades ago are a popular one. Since the sexual revolution of the 1960s, Americans just aren't seeing church as an important part of their lives. Some conservative churches have given Christianity a bad name, what with all their war-mongering, anti-immigration, misogynistic vitriol. All that anti-gay marriage, pray-the-gay-away stuff drove people away. Televangelists really soured people on Christianity, with all their corruption and hoarding wealth and acting like they could heal people over the TV airwaves. After years of being unwilling to accept science, the church just lost all credibility. It's not socially advantageous to be Christian anymore, and most of the so-called Christians were just doing it for that reason, so now they're leaving the church. And don't let's forget the Crusades.

All of these theories have evidence to back them up. It is true that American churches have been in decline since around the 60s. It is true that many of these issues have contributed to that decline.

THESE REASONS MATTER, BUT NOT AS MUCH AS YOU THINK

Research shows us that if you follow up with first-time visitors in a personal manner within the first 24 hours of their visit, there is a 70% chance of them coming back, and almost zero if you don't follow up at all. So if first-time visitors regularly come to our church, and we don't ever follow up with them, and they never come back, can we really pin that on the Crusades?

If your members are regularly out in the community but never, ever mention their church and so are never, ever able to have a conversation where they might be able to invite someone, is that really the fault of the Catholic priests who abused children back in the 1940s?

I think that the declining local church has a problem, but it's not what we all think. I think that the global church has a problem, and we are caught between a rock and a hard place. On the one hand, we personally didn't necessarily cause the problem, but at the same time it is up to us to solve it if we are to move forward.

THE INTEGRITY DICHOTOMY IS A REAL THING ON MANY LEVELS

I talk a lot about integrity in churches and in individuals. I speak of integrity not as a moral measuring stick for judgment, but as a way of ascertaining unity and consistency. Unfortunately, the church has an integrity problem on many levels.

On the global level, churches have done some pretty horrific things, historically. This causes an integrity problem because the church simultaneously purports to be a moral authority. People see this and smell hypocrisy.

At the same time, churches are in disagreement. There are conservative churches condemning gays to hell and progressive churches that were performing gay marriages and fighting for equal rights decades before they became legal. Some use the claim that America is a Christian nation in order to disenfranchise Jews and Muslims. Others claim that Jesus welcomed the stranger and declare their churches sanctuaries to immigrants and refugees. To the outside observer, it would appear that "the church" has two diametrically opposed interpretations of the Bible and belief systems based on it.

This is a problem. I would love to say that the solution is for everyone just to agree and subscribe to one single unified way of thinking, but that would not only be impossible, it would defy both historical and biblical precedents. Despite what the Catholic Church may have us believe, there have always been differing sects of Christianity that had very different takes on the scripture and Jesus and theology.

To people with little understanding of history, scripture, theology, or the various denominations, who are watching as these arguments continue to play out in their newsfeed on a global and national scale, it appears that the church can't really get its act together. As a result, many shy away from Christianity and religion altogether, and who can blame them?

As progressive Christians, we are acutely aware of this dichotomy. We are sensitive to the notion of hypocrisy. We are painfully cognizant of the way that all Christians—no matter how progressive—have been accused of association with some of the worst perpetrators of human rights violations throughout history. We know from experience that once we mention that we are Christians, once we let it be known that we attend church, we may be subject to sweeping judgments about what we believe, whom we have harmed, and how we may be disenfranchising people across the nation and around the world right now. If we are not skilled debaters, if we do not have at-your-fingertips recall of scripture and history, and most importantly, if we do not have the time—because conversations of this nature require enormous amounts of time and patience—there can be no resolution. And we are left with one more person who is angry at the church.

As a result, progressive Christians have their own integrity problem in their own local churches. Our desire not to be perceived as anything like a conservative Christian, avoid conflict, and exude respectful acceptance leads us to do things that are inconsistent and counter-productive. We say we want to welcome the stranger, but we avoid approaching newcomers for fear of being perceived as a "Bible thumper." We say we want our churches to grow, but go decades without ever inviting anyone to church. We spend enormous amounts of time, energy, and money on outreach programs and marketing programs to let people know how *attractive* we are as a church, without actually engaging with anyone on a meaningful level.

We know that our churches are different, we know that we have a lot to offer, we know that we have a long and impressive history of accomplishments in the community, biblical literacy, and close and healthy relationships. But we don't tell anyone because we don't want to risk a negative reaction. The number of progressive churches that self-describe as their town's "best kept secret" would astound you. This phrase in and of itself is a dichotomy. If they are the absolute best example of Christianity that the town has to offer, then why doesn't anyone know about it or talk about it?

Christianity is in decline. The progressive local church is in decline. These are facts that cannot be denied. And yet they are not the final word. Because despite all this, most progressive churches still get a steady stream of one to two first-time visitors per week. And when the Christian Church in the United States appears to be behaving at its worst—mixing Church and State, disenfranchising the LGBT Community, Muslims, immigrants and women, condoning child abuse and sexual assault, racism and police brutality—more and more people in the United States are seeking out their local progressive churches looking for answers, community, and a way to make a difference.

HOLDING DICHOTOMY IN TENSION AND MOVING FORWARD

There is a hard reality here, but we must name it if we are to be able to make any effective growth effort. There are several dichotomies that must be embraced:

The Church Universal has an integrity problem that absolutely affects church decline across the nation. At the same time, you can still have a successful growth strategy in your local church.

If your local church is in decline, you may have an integrity problem in your own personal (yes, you, the person reading this right now) approach to first-time visitors and people you could invite in the community. This does not mean that you are morally bereft, only that what you are wanting and what you are doing are not in alignment. At the same time, this does not mean that you can't start to turn it around in a single week.

You have very little—if any—control over the history of abuses that have given the Church Universal a black eye, and you have very little—if any—power right now to tackle the nationwide issues that are causing people to question the church's integrity. At the same time, you have every single tool you need to be able to begin to restore it.

You did not necessarily cause the integrity mess that the Church Universal suffers from right now. At the same time, it is your responsibility to clean it up.

So what do we do when we are faced with such dichotomies? What do we do when we are powerless over problems bigger than us? What do we do when we are caught between a rock and a hard place with no good options going forward? What do we do when we have all the responsibility to fix something, but none of the authority to actually do it?

REMEMBERING WHO IS IN CHARGE

The answer is simple. We remember that we are not in charge. We remember that our God is bigger than all this. We remember that when the Roman Empire and Jerusalem were in this very same situation—filled with corruption, rife with human rights abuses, violent to the point of death—the disciples thought that it was all over when Jesus was crucified. They hid their faith, they pretended they didn't know Him, they all but gave up the fight for the homeless, the hungry, the widow, the orphan, the stranger, the sick, and the poor. But three days later God responded, and when Jesus rose from the tomb we knew that God was bigger than corruption, bigger than all the human rights abuses, bigger than violence, bigger than death. On that day, God said "no." Jesus urged and commissioned the disciples to carry on the work that He had begun, and they had to trust that God would give them the tools they needed to carry it out. We remember that God has been an agent throughout history to act in ways that were bigger than the evils of the day, bigger than the powers-that-be.

We are in the same position today, but sometimes we progressives forget who is in charge. We work so hard on all of the issues facing the world—and it is difficult and exhausting work—that we forget that it's not all up to us. We forget that God can find a way where we cannot. We forget that God can create elegant solutions to the most impossible problems. We forget that we are but vessels and one small part of the much larger body of Christ. We forget that Jesus said, "Come to me, all you that are weary and are carrying heavy burdens, and I will give you rest. Take my yoke upon you, and learn from me; for I am gentle and humble in heart, and you will find rest for your souls" (Matthew 11:28-29).

A DAILY PRAYER

Starting right now, I want you to turn this problem over to God. Turn your church over to God. Turn this entire overwhelming problem over to God. This is a simple prayer that I have used for many years, and I invite you to say it right now and every day while we go through this process. Screenshot it so that you can have it at your fingertips.

"Loving God, this is your church. I can't grow it by myself so I am casting this burden on you and I ask that you grow it. If there is something you want me to do to help then let me know. Be sure to make it really, really clear so that I don't miss it. Amen."

Pay attention over the next few days and see what you notice.

3

RESEARCH VERSUS RESULTS

$\mathcal{A}$fter I had attended my home church in Portland, Oregon for a few years, I happened to find myself in the foyer one day and spotted the guestbook. Swept up with a bit of nostalgia, I went to see if I could find my entry from the first time I had visited. As I leafed through the book, I saw my name and many others. I was amazed to discover that the guestbook held names of first-time visitors going back twenty years. I was startled when I realized that that entire twenty years was encompassed in only the first four pages. The rest of the book was empty. This was astounding because we had a steady stream of one to two visitors per week, but they clearly weren't signing the book and they weren't coming back.

That night I happened to be on the phone with my mother, and I told her my worries and what I had noticed. She said, "Yes, that reminds me of how my church used to be when I started attending." My mouth dropped. My mother's church, the one I had been raised in, was a thriving church with three standing-room-only Sunday morning services, two choirs, a youth group that always numbered in the 30s, and dozens of community ministries. I tried to imagine it one-quarter full. I tried to imagine only the same two children going up to have the Children's Moment with the pastor every single week. They would have looked so tiny in that big, empty space. I couldn't picture it. "... that is," she said, "until Myrtle took it upon herself to run around with the guestbook every single Sunday after church and got all the visitors to sign it." I remembered Myrtle, the 80-something, tiny woman with a perpetual scowl on her face and a determined walk. Really? She had done all that?

Something clicked in me that day. I realized I had nothing to lose and everything to gain.

Over the next few weeks I watched the greeters at the front door in order to try and solve this mystery, and here is what I discovered. The foyer was between the church's outer doors and the sanctuary doors. The guestbook was on its own pedestal in the corner to the right of the sanctuary doors. When newcomers came in the outer doors, greeters would welcome them warmly and ask them if this was their first time visiting. This was merely a formality, as the church was small enough that everybody knew everybody and any visitors were easily identified. When the visitors affirmed that they were, indeed, there for the first time, the greeters would invite them to please sign the guestbook and point to it on the other side of the room in the corner, about eight feet from the doors that led to the sanctuary. Then the greeters would turn to the next person coming in. Very few visitors ever made it that far. Very few ever received a warm, welcoming, personal letter like the one that I received. And even fewer had a neighbor like Mollie with them who would take them by the arm and introduce them to everyone.

I began taking the guestbook and a pen around after worship and asking first-time visitors to sign the guestbook. I would make a point of asking them to leave their contact information so that the minister could follow up with them. I also took the time to chat with them and get to know them a little, and then sent them a personal, hand-written card that said how nice it was to get to meet them and that I looked forward to continuing our conversation. I would let the minister know whenever there was a new signature in the guestbook, and pass along anything it would be important for her/him to know when he reached out to him, i.e. if they were new in town, if there was a serious illness in the family, if they had children, etc.

People started coming back, and the church started to grow. One of my most surprising Sundays was when a visitor returned. He had made a point of saying he popped into several different services and wanted to make it clear that he had no intention of joining anywhere. He appeared the following Sunday and walked right up to me with my card in his hand and said, "I got your card! I'm back! I'm looking forward to continuing our conversation, as well!" Six months later, he and his wife joined the church.

There are three things I want to point out about this method. First, it cost nothing (except for a postage stamp). Second, I didn't have to ask anyone's—or any committee's—permission to do it. Third, it was extremely effective.

At that seminarian's conference years ago, I learned that if you respond with a personal follow-up within twenty-four hours of a newcomer's first-time visit to your church, there is a 70% chance that they will return. A personal follow-up can be a hand-written card or a personal—not form—letter from the minister, a loaf of bread on their doorstep, or a phone call. I've even heard of some churches dropping homemade apple pies on newcomers' doorsteps, but I've never tried that myself. The exact nature of the follow-up isn't so important, and every church has their own individual tradition and flair. What is important is that it happens within twenty-four hours, which for a Sunday morning visitor means Monday afternoon at the latest. If visitors are coming for other midweek events, the same 24-hour rule applies.

Research shows us that if you give that same exact personal follow-up—a phone call, note, loaf of bread, etc.—on Wednesday, there is less than a 50% chance that the newcomer will return. If you give the exact same personal follow-up on Friday, there is less than a 20% chance that the newcomer will return. If there is zero follow-up, there is a 0% chance that they will return.

If churches do not collect contact information from their visitors, there is a 0% chance that they will be able to follow up, which means that there is a 0% chance of their visitors returning.

Over the years I have tried different approaches to newcomers and different approaches to following up with them within twenty-four hours. I discovered that simply calling them got pretty good results. However, as I refined my approach I discovered that by approaching visitors with a particular method, I was able to successfully invite a high number of them out for a meeting over a cup of coffee shortly after their first visit. This coffee meeting—which we will discuss in detail later—allowed me to get to know them better and get them involved with the church in a meaningful way much more quickly.

My first full-time position after I graduated from seminary was an interim position, where I spent two and a half years. I put all of these methods to the test and tracked the numbers. We had about one to two visitors per week, totaling 90 first-time visitors in about a year.

88% (79) of first-time visitors returned the following Sunday.

50% (45) of the first-time visitors became actively involved in the church. This led our monthly worship to go from 45 on a Sunday to between 55 and 60. I define "actively involved" as:

1. Attending church at least twice a month.
2. Donating generously (at least $100 per month)
3. Actively participating in at least one other ministry besides attending Sunday worship, i.e. volunteering at the food pantry, singing in the choir, helping prepare meals for the monthly homeless shelter dinner we supported, attending the weekly Bible Study class, etc.

20% (18) of the first-time visitors joined the church.

Let me reiterate that this cost the church very little. This was also done during the interim period when the church was in-between settled pastors, which allowed the church to build an upward momentum. The budget, attendance, and membership grew, which allowed the church to be able to hire a full-time minister and attract a higher-quality minister, as they were a more attractive church. This methodology was extremely effective.

Since then I have moved to a full-time settled position and hosted many workshops and consulted with many churches. The churches that have applied this methodology and tracked their numbers have seen visitors return at rates between 85% and 91%. My rate has—amazingly—remained steady at 88%.

It is easy for churches to feel overwhelmed and paralyzed as they see numbers decline, populations age, and visitors never come back. By taking the simple steps in this book, you can start to turn the paralysis into action, first-time visitors into long-term members, and a declining church into a thriving one.

4

FEAR IS AT THE HEART OF IT ALL

I once led a strategic planning session for a church that wanted to grow. The congregation was brainstorming strategies for bringing newcomers into church, and one lady suggested implementing "Ask-a-Friend Sunday." She had seen it used at a different church. The strategy was to plan a Sunday and announce it weeks in advance. On that particular Sunday everyone in the congregation was encouraged to invite a friend. The beauty of the plan was its simplicity. If every person in the congregation invites a friend, then the attendance that Sunday will double. I asked her how often they had held "Ask-a-Friend Sunday," and she said they had been hosting it twice a year for the past seven years or so. I asked how many people had actually brought a friend on any of those Sundays. She seemed a little embarrassed to report that the number was zero. Not a single person had ever brought a friend on any of the designated Sundays. She said that she had followed up with the members to find out why, and they all said they were too scared to talk to their friends about church.

When I am leading workshops on newcomer retention, I always begin with a visioning exercise. I would invite you to do the same. Close your eyes and imagine that you are in your sanctuary. Imagine that you are there on a Sunday morning, a few minutes before worship is going to begin. The music director is playing in the background, the choir is warming up. People are hustling and bustling to light candles, set out flowers, arrange the communion table. People are filtering in and finding their seats. Amidst all of this, you see a visitor that has never come before step through the doors at the back of the sanctuary. Envision yourself walking up to them, introducing yourself, and asking them for their contact information so that you can follow up with them. Sit with that feeling for a long minute. Notice how you feel about that, and where you feel it in your body. Lay your hand on the part of your body where you feel that sensation.

Whenever I do this exercise, the majority of the participants lay their hands across their stomach. A few will lay their hands on their forehead. Often, at least one person will grab their throat. Gut pain, headache, trouble breathing. These are signs of anxiety and fear. In general, people in progressive churches don't like approaching newcomers—let alone asking for their contact information—because it terrifies them. If you are like most of the people who have participated in this exercise, you are feeling fear as well.

Before we can learn about how to approach a newcomer, we must address the fears that prevent us from doing so. In my experience, even if people memorize a simple script that they can use, they will not use it out of fear. Just as people didn't bring a friend to "Ask-a-Friend Sunday" because they were too afraid to say, "Would you like to come to church with me on Sunday?" we can't begin to learn *what* to say to newcomers until we learn *why* we are unable to talk with them in the first place.

These are the most common things that people say they are afraid of when I ask them *why* they felt pain in their gut, or felt their throat close, or felt their head start to hurt:

1. We don't want to be perceived as pushy or aggressive.
2. We don't want to be like those conservative evangelicals, bible-thumpers, religious nut jobs, etc. who force their religion on people.
3. We don't want to invade their privacy.
4. We should at least wait until the end of the service or until we get to know them better before we ask them something like that.
5. They will probably say no because they think we are going to spam them or something.
6. They might say no and reject us!
7. They will feel a lot of tension and discomfort in this awkward situation.
8. It's not my job—the minister/lay leader/moderator/anyone else but me—should do this.

Let's go through these one at a time.

WE DON'T WANT TO BE PERCEIVED AS PUSHY OR AGGRESSIVE

I invite you to remember a time when you were new. Perhaps you were starting at a new job or at a new school. Perhaps you were just going to your first day at high school, where you didn't know a lot of the people there. I invite you to remember what it was like to get there on your very first day. You probably had to go to bed earlier the night before than you normally would have. You probably had to get up earlier than you normally would have. You had to worry about what you were going to wear, with little or no instruction—Casual? Formal? Somewhere in-between? Are jeans OK? What about sneakers? Heels? Would a button-down shirt stand out? Would a tie? You had to get there early enough that you weren't late. You had to get there late enough that you weren't standing around feeling awkward for 20 minutes. You had to figure out directions, and you likely had to figure out where to park. You had to figure out where to enter the building, and where within the building you had to go first. You had to get to the room and size up the seating arrangements, not knowing whether everything was assigned or whether it was open. Do you sit all the way in the front so you can see but risk a lot of attention, or all the way in the back to remain relatively anonymous but risk not being able to see or hear or participate? Remember how much trouble—physical and emotional—you had to go through to get there.

This is what newcomers go through the first time they come to your church. In addition to all of this, many of them carry emotional or physical trauma from churches they used to attend, so that also adds a layer of tension to their experience.

Now, imagine what it would feel like if you spent several hours there and no one said anything to you the whole time. Imagine what it would feel like to leave, not knowing anyone's name and no one knowing yours. Would your first thought be, "I am sure glad those folks weren't pushy or aggressive!" Likely not.

Now, remember what it was like that time when someone smiled at you and motioned you over to sit next to them. Maybe offered you a gummy bear from the bag they were munching on or a pencil because they knew you would need one. Perhaps they gave you a heads-up that the teacher always calls on the kids in the front row or gives a pop quiz every Thursday on the assigned readings. Remember what a relief and a joy it was to know you had a friend on the first day.

At my first call, when I started we had approximately 45 attend on a Sunday, but 18 joined the first year I was there. Many more expressed their wish to stay, and were adamant that there was a *moment* when they knew this was the right church for them. It generally occurred within the first two weeks of attending. When I asked them why they decided to stay, they generally gave two answers.

Approximately 50% said that it was because somethi
wrong during the worship service and everyone was cool .
And this was true. At that church, something went wrong nearly
every Sunday. The microphones would screech, or the slide
machine would suddenly turn itself off and need five minutes to
reboot. The wrong words would be printed for the hymns, or the
lengthy and scripted communion service would be missing the
first page at the altar. Because this church had a history of tension,
splitting, and controlling and toxic personalities—all of which had
actually erupted even during worship services—I made a
conscious commitment to roll with the flow no matter what
happened. So whenever something went wrong, I would laugh,
tell everyone not to worry, make an on-the-fly adjustment to the
service, and keep on going. Newcomers told me repeatedly that
when those situations happened on their first Sunday, *they knew
that that church was a safe place to be yourself, even if you weren't
perfect.*

The other 50% said that they had been church shopping. They
had attended eight or so different churches over eight weeks, and
at every one they had filled out the pew pad, the welcome card or
the guestbook. They had filled it out completely with their
contact information and put it where instructed—in the collection plate or into a box, sometimes even into an usher's hand.
Without fail, they would say, "You were the only church that
called me back, so I knew you cared." That cannot be emphasized
enough: First, *we were the only church that called them back.* Most
churches don't call people back. Each time, at least seven other
churches in town had had them visit, had their contact information, and *didn't call them back. Second, when we called them back, they
knew we cared.* The newcomers equated the personal follow-up not
with pushiness or aggression, but with *caring.*

By *not* calling them, other churches sent a very clear message:
We don't care.

By calling them, we sent a very clear message: We care.

After they had had seven separate first days in a new place, with all of the physical and emotional turmoil those entailed *each time*, the messages they received were amplified. In my experience, people *want* to be contacted. They want to know you care. It makes them feel accepted to know that someone went to the trouble to reach out to them after they went to so much trouble to come visit in the first place.

Consider the fallout that happens when we don't follow up with our first-time visitors. They think we don't care, and after several church visits, they start to wonder what is wrong with them. Churches watch first-time visitors come and never return, and after months of this happening, start to wonder what is wrong with them. Stop the madness!

WE DON'T WANT TO BE LIKE THOSE CONSERVATIVE EVANGELICALS, BIBLE-THUMPERS, RELIGIOUS NUT JOBS, ETC. WHO FORCE THEIR RELIGION ON PEOPLE

Oftentimes, when we talk about asking a newcomer for their contact information, or following up with them in any way, we conjure up images of televangelists. Progressive Christians often erroneously equate this with chasing people down and asking if they have a moment to talk about Jesus.

Very often, progressive Christians assume that approaching a newcomer to welcome them and ask to follow up with them is the same as trying to convert them on the spot, which would definitely be trying to force your religion on someone and would most certainly qualify as pushy. What we are learning in this book is the opposite of this. What we are learning is how to be the kind of church that is safe and healthy, honors boundaries, and has integrity. When we approach newcomers in that very first interaction, we are doing more than asking for a phone number. *We are beginning to rebuild the integrity that has been lost and healing the wounds that have been caused by the church.*

When we ask a newcomer for contact information, we are doing it for two reasons: so that we can get to know them better and answer any questions they may have. When we begin learning the script in Chapter Four, we will come back again and again to the concept of integrity. By integrity, I mean when your thoughts, words, and actions are all in alignment. We will tell newcomers what we are going to do, and then keep our word.

The problem that a lot of progressives (and I) have with some conservative churches and with televangelists, or with any of the religious institutions, is not necessarily their theology—though there may be some disagreement with it—it is their lack of integrity. For example, if a church asks you to sign their guest-book because you are visiting, and then puts you onto a mailing list and spams you with unwanted email without asking your permission to add you to these lists, then they are *saying* one thing and *doing* another. If a person with a megaphone shouts at you that Jesus loves you and you should come to Jesus and Jesus died for you because he loved the world so much, but wears a sign listing all of the people whom Jesus hates (and you or your family members or friends identify as one of the items on the list), then they are saying two conflicting things, and lack integrity. If a tele-vangelist asks you to send him your prayers in the mail so that he can pray for you, but then throws the prayers away and instead uses your contact information to repeatedly ask you for money using coercive and guilt-inducing tactics, then he is *saying* one thing while *thinking* and *doing* another. He lacks integrity. If a church gives you a welcome card that asks you for your contact information so that they can follow up with you and then never does, they are *saying* one thing and *doing* another. They lack integrity. Lack of integrity is palpable in a church. Breaking someone's trust the very first time they visit is almost irreparable. With the enormous integrity problem that the church is suffering from right now, when someone walks into a church for the first time, they are already a little skeptical, and rightfully so.

By *saying* what you are *thinking* and then *following through* by *doing* the same thing that you *said* you would, you are demonstrating integrity. In my experience, approaching newcomers and asking for contact information in the manner that I detail in Chapter Four is a breath of fresh air for newcomers. It begins to heal old wounds, begins to assure them that this church is a safe place that honors boundaries, accepts them exactly as they are, has integrity, and replaces skepticism with trust.

WE DON'T WANT TO INVADE THEIR PRIVACY

Invasion of privacy suggests that we forcibly extract their contact information, or that we use it to contact them against their will. This is the opposite of what we are doing. We are not going to show up at their house uninvited, or put them onto our email newsletter without expressly asking permission. We are not going to call them at all hours of the night or try to steal their identity. We are not asking them to tell us their social security number or the PIN number for their debit card. We are not trying to coerce them to tell us their mother's maiden name or how old they were when they lost their virginity. We are not planning to peek into their windows or track their movements. We do not want to know where their children go to school or how many bite-sized Snickers they consume when they think no one is looking. We are not going to take embarrassing pictures of them and post them on Facebook. Our goal is very aboveboard and straightforward: to get to know them better and answer any questions they may have in a casual meeting where we have time to talk with them. Our script explicitly tells them exactly what we are going to do with their contact information *before* we even ask for it, so that they can make an informed decision as to whether or not they want to give us their contact information.

Many folks assume that simply by asking them for contact information we are invading their privacy, but in fact we are not.

We are demonstrating honesty and integrity by telling them what we would like to do, respectfully asking their permission, giving them space to think about it, and respecting their decision, *whatever it may be.*

WE SHOULD AT LEAST WAIT UNTIL THE END OF THE SERVICE OR UNTIL WE GET TO KNOW THEM BETTER BEFORE WE ASK THEM SOMETHING LIKE THAT

I will let you in on a secret that most people don't know about first-time visitors to churches. They have superpowers. No, seriously, they do. Really. Ask anyone who has tried to catch up with a newcomer right after service so they can say hello, only to find that they are nowhere to be found, and no one knows where they went.

First of all, newcomers can walk through walls. I cannot tell you how many times I have missed talking with a newcomer at the beginning of worship when they arrived, processed down the aisle to the back of the sanctuary during the closing hymn, and greeted every single person that came out of the church right in front of me, only to find that the newcomer had disappeared. Since there is only one main exit, the only conceivable explanation is that they walked through a wall to get out of the sanctuary without being seen, noticed, or greeted.

Second, newcomers can make paper disappear into thin air. If you give a newcomer a welcome card and ask them to fill it out and return it to you, they will make it disappear. Even if they promise to fill it out and put it in the collection plate, they will make it disappear. Even if they start filling it out and get halfway done before you walk away, it will disappear into thin air. Even if as they are leaving they shake your hand and swear that they completed the form, made sure to include both their phone number and email address, and point to the usher they handed it to across the room, it will disappear into thin air. Even if you see

29

them at the guestbook actually writing and their name is on it with a big "Thank you!" and a smiley face, their address and phone number will have disappeared off the page. Even if they look you in the eye and tell you that they filled out every visitor form, pew pad and guestbook with their contact information at the last seven churches they visited and they are really upset that no one called them back, and even if you promise them you will call them if they just give you the card at the end of worship, if you walk away without *your* church's completed visitor card, it will disappear without a trace.

In my experience, visitors generally come in during the last two minutes before worship starts. They time it that way so that they are not late, but so that neither are they so early that they have to sit around awkwardly staring at the walls or other people that they don't know. So it is hard to have a meaningful conversation with them at the beginning of worship. I understand your dilemma, I really do. It feels a lot safer to wait for them to wander into the coffee hour *after* worship where you can casually chat with them about the weather, where they're from, what they do for a living, how the 49ers are doing in the playoffs, the price of tea in China, and then casually work the conversation around to maybe following up with them. Except that now that you have had such a nice conversation, you won't feel the need to follow up with them because you assume that, having established a *rapport*, they will naturally gravitate back the following Sunday. So you don't go so far as to follow up.

In my experience, if we don't get the contact information in our hands at the beginning of worship service, we don't get it at all. Again, if we don't get any contact information, there is a 0% possibility of us following up. If we don't follow up, there is a 0% chance they will return.

While it is very tempting to wait until the end of worship service, it is critical that we get the contact information at the beginning of worship service. It is critical that we sit and wait while they fill out the card or spell out their email address or sign the guest book so that we can be sure we have it *before* worship starts.

People often ask how this is possible, as the last two minutes before worship service are the busiest time, when the minister is most distracted. If a newcomer arrives when the beginning of worship is imminent, I make eye contact with my music director or liturgist. I hold up two fingers and mouth the words, "Two minutes." This means, "Keep vamping the music for two minutes because I am talking with a newcomer and that is more important than starting worship on time today." Now I can imagine that many of you reading this book just had a case of vapors. Go ahead and breathe deeply. Use a paper bag if you need to. Drink a glass of water. Put your head between your legs until your vision clears. When you are feeling better, allow me to explain my thinking.

Churches are in decline, and they are in decline for many reasons. Most likely, you are reading this book because your church is in decline. There are many, many reasons why churches are in decline. But the two most effective ways to overcome the decline and get your church growing are to 1) train your congregation to invite their friends and acquaintances to church and 2) to stop letting first-time visitors be one-time visitors. If you are not following up with every single first-time visitor within 24 hours, then you are allowing them to slip away quite unnecessarily. As long as you continue to do this, your church will continue to decline. If you take the easier path—let worship start on time, try to catch the newcomer after worship and miss them, as a consequence have zero follow-up with them, thus resulting in a 0% chance that they will ever return—your church will continue to decline.

If, however, you start worship two minutes late that day, but follow up with the newcomer the following day, there is between a 70% and 91.4% chance that they will return, and a 50% chance that they will keep coming and get involved. They will bring new life and ideas to your ministries, donate generously, and increase your worship attendance by continuing to attend and inviting their friends. And all it cost you was two minutes that most folks likely didn't notice anyway. Spending two minutes of your time and starting worship two minutes late is *absolutely worth your time* because it is a solid investment in your church's future.

THEY WILL PROBABLY SAY NO BECAUSE THEY THINK WE ARE GOING TO SPAM THEM OR SOMETHING

We are not going to spam them. If you are the type of church that spams people, then stop. But in my experience most progressive churches don't spam people. They may have a monthly or weekly newsletter that comes out via email or snail mail, but there is no excessive contact. During the coffee meeting I tell them that we have a newsletter, how often it comes out, and via which method, and ask if I may have their permission to add them to the list so that they can be informed about upcoming events. Then I respect their decision, *whatever it may be.*

Again, this is about integrity. Our goal is simple: we want to get to know them better and answer any questions they may have. In order to do this, we need their contact information. We do not need to spam them, we do not want to spam them. By being clear about our intentions and then honoring them, most people are willing to give us our contact information.

THEY MIGHT SAY NO AND REJECT US!

This is true! This one is actually a very real fear that might actually happen. Sometimes people say no. But in my experience, nineteen out of twenty people say *yes.* In my experience, the one who says no has usually already decided that they are not interested in attending the church anymore. Just their initial gut instinct has already told them that this is not the right place for them, and it has nothing to do with you. It may be the smell of the incense that reminds them of some unpleasant childhood memory. It may be that the music is not what they were expecting. It may be that by glancing through the program they realize that your church is at theological odds with their belief system. It may be that while they could never articulate why, your church just doesn't *feel right*. So when you ask them for their contact information, they will look uncomfortable and tell you that no, they would just rather not, right now. Likely, they will leave directly after worship and you will never see them again.

This is totally fine! One church will never meet the needs of all people. There will always be some folk for whom your church is not a good fit, and their needs will be better met elsewhere. So let's get this out of the way right now. If you approach a newcomer for their contact information and they tell you no, then smile and say,

"Thank you for telling me, that's why we ask!"

Take a big breath, really think about what this tells someone. You thank them for being honest with you and tell them that hearing their genuine response, their honest opinion, their real feelings on the subject is why you ask in the first place. Even if they say no, you are still sending a clear message that this church is a safe place that honors boundaries and has integrity. So memorize this line now and practice it often. Be ready to bust it out if you need it. Most likely, nineteen out of twenty times you won't need it. But in case you do, say it with sincerity, because we really are genuinely interested in respecting people's feelings and boundaries, and their being honest with you is a gift.

Now try it again with a warm invitation:

"Thank you for telling me, that's why we ask. I sure hope you'll come back again soon so that we can get to know you better."

Again, whether people say yes or no, we have one goal, and their refusal to give contact information does not change that. They may close the door, but we will leave it open. One of the best rejections I ever received was from a woman who said that she knew after one visit that we were definitely not the church for her, but that she really appreciated the welcome—it was one of the warmest and friendliest she had ever experienced.

THEY WILL FEEL A LOT OF TENSION AND DISCOMFORT IN THIS AWKWARD SITUATION

This is a projection. We have already established that the newcomer wants to be asked. Nineteen out of twenty of them are happy you asked and will give you their contact information. They see it as a message that you care.

The only person who may be feeling uncomfortable in this situation is the asker. You. The person who grabs their stomach or has trouble breathing or feels a tension headache just thinking about it. When people say, "The newcomer will feel a lot of tension and discomfort," what they really mean is, "I will feel a lot of tension and discomfort, so I assume the newcomer will feel the same way." I want to encourage you to recognize that the discomfort is all in your own mind, not in the mind of the person being asked. Take some deep breaths and allow yourself to feel what the newcomer is feeling: relief that someone is coming to say hello, and a warm and surprising gratitude that your church cares. Here is a prayer that I used to say right before I approached a newcomer, often as I was walking over to them:

Loving God, help me to stay calm. Help me to say everything that needs to be said. Help me to hear everything that needs to be heard. Help me to be a true reflection of your love, your light, and your radical welcome to this new person. Amen.

IT'S NOT MY JOB—THE MINISTER/LAY
LEADER/MODERATOR/ANYONE ELSE BUT ME—SHOULD
DO THIS.

"One of the scribes came near and heard them disputing with one another, and seeing that he answered them well, he asked him, "Which commandment is the first of all?" Jesus answered, "The first is, 'Hear, O Israel: the Lord our God, the Lord is one; you shall love the Lord your God with all your heart, and with all your soul, and with all your mind, and with all your strength.' The second is this, *You shall love your neighbor as yourself.*' There is no other commandment greater than these" (Mark 12:28-31, NRSV).

"When the Son of Man comes in his glory, and all the angels with him, then he will sit on the throne of his glory. All the nations will be gathered before him, as he will separate people one from another as a shepherd separates the sheep from the goats, and he will put the sheep at his right hand and the goats at the left. Then the king will say to those at his right hand, 'Come, you that are blessed by my Father, inherit the kingdom prepared for you from the foundation of the world; for I was hungry and you gave me food, I was thirsty and you gave me something to drink, *I was a stranger and you welcomed me...*'" (Matthew 25:31-35).

"The alien who resides with you shall be to you as the citizen among you; *you shall love the alien as yourself,* for you were aliens in the land of Egypt: I am the LORD your God" (Leviticus 19:34, NRSV).

"You shall also love the stranger, for you were strangers in the land of Egypt" (Deuteronomy 10:19, NRSV).

"Let mutual love continue. *Do not neglect to show hospitality to strangers,* for by doing that some have entertained angels without knowing it" (Hebrews 13:1, NRSV) [emphasis mine].

There are numerous passages throughout both the Hebrew Bible and the New Testament that command us to welcome the stranger, and in none of them is there a disclaimer, "So long as you are either the ordained minister or Chair of the Welcoming Committee at a church."

When I began approaching people with the guestbook years ago, I did it because no one else was doing it. It needed to be done, so it became my job. Simply by reading this book, knowing what you now know about how much this job needs to be done, it is now your job. Once you learn how to do it, it will become even more of your job because it needs to be done well. If you are the minister at your church, it is now your job. If you are the head of the Hospitality Team, it is now your job. If you are an usher or greeter, it is now your job. If you are simply a person who casually attends, not even yet officially a member, it is now your job. You may be feeling a strong resistance to this, because you don't want to do it. It makes you feel uncomfortable. You already do a lot. You already do so much. You already do too much. You can think of at least three other people in your church to whom this should really be assigned. You can think of a lot of other things you might do to help grow your church which don't require interacting with newcomers—let alone asking them for their contact information! It is still your job.

You may be envisioning fliers, or ads in the newspaper or telephone book, or a really neato new sign on the side of the building. Or a movie night, or an engaging new book study. Perhaps you could give the Sunday school room a fresh coat of paint and some brightly colored new toys. This is all avoidance. These are all things that progressive Christians do to try and avoid the one thing that will be most effective in keeping people coming back, but that makes them the most uncomfortable.

Learn to recognize that this intense discomfort and avoidance is evidence of a growing edge that you need to work on. Not your church, in a long committee exploration—you. You personally.

Because this is your job and nobody is going to do it but you. And it has to be done, or your church will continue to decline.

A perfect example of all of these wrapped up in one was a question that someone brought up at a recent workshop. A woman asked me what I thought of an idea that her newly-formed Hospitality Committee had come up with to get newcomers to return to church. She said something like this:

"The idea is to make a visitor bag. It would be a tote bag that is really decorated—you know, with lots of glitter on it and bright colors so that it really stands out so that everyone in the church knows that the person holding it is a newcomer so that they will want to go over and say hello to them. And inside there would be some home-baked cookies or treats and fliers for upcoming events for our church so that they will have a reason to come back. What do you think? Will it work?"

This is an excellent example of what churches usually do to address the fears they don't even really realize they have. In this example, we can see fear of violating social expectations, fear of rejection, and avoidance all wrapped up in one.

If your church is considering something like this—and I have seen some very involved welcome packets—I will tell you the same thing I told this woman. There are three reasons, she says, why they are developing this visitor bag:

1. To identify visitors to members of their congregation
2. To give newcomers a reason to come back
3. To make members of their congregation want to go over and greet the newcomer

Here's the problem with all three of these reasons:

1. TO IDENTIFY VISITORS TO MEMBERS OF THEIR CONGREGATION

In churches with fewer than 100 people attending on a Sunday, first-time visitors are not hard to spot. In these churches, the people attending have been attending for a long time and already know everybody by sight. When a first-time visitor comes in, *everybody* knows that they are new. There is not one person in that church that is not cognizant of the fact that a newcomer is in their midst. Making the first-time visitor carry around a sparkly bag as identification is superfluous and—dare I say—ridiculous.

2. TO GIVE NEWCOMERS A REASON TO COME BACK

On the surface, it makes sense that a newcomer might take that glittery bag home, pull out all of the information, read through it, identify one or two upcoming events that they might like to attend, and then return. But the reality is that that doesn't often happen. First of all, they already went to all the psychological trouble of coming for the first time and no one said hello to them. Just to be clear, this would be especially noticeable because everyone in the church clearly knew each other and were greeting one another. Why would they go to all the trouble of going through the first-time experience again when the first one was so painful? Second, let us remember that research shows us that it is the personal follow-up that makes the difference between returning and not returning, NOT the package they receive during their visit.

3. TO MAKE MEMBERS OF THEIR CONGREGATION WANT TO GO OVER AND GREET THE NEWCOMER

Herein lies the crux of the problem. It was very subtle the way the woman described the purpose of the bag, but the reality is that she and her committee are not only trying to get newcomers to return, they are trying to get their congregation to greet newcomers, which they are clearly not doing. If the entire congregation is having trouble greeting newcomers because of their own discomfort, then creating a brightly-colored sparkling glitter bag full of cookies is not going to help this situation.

The glitter bag is a wonderful example of how much trouble churches will go to, and how much money they will spend to avoid doing the one thing Jesus calls us to do, and that will be one of the most effective tools in growing our churches. It would keep many people in their church busy shopping for supplies and crafting, baking and photocopying. They could create a budget item around it and label it "Outreach." They could look with deep satisfaction on a whole table covered with brightly-colored, sparkling bags near their church entrance, and the whole spectacle would likely brighten up their day. In the end, they could track all of the hours and dollars that they had spent and assume that they had done their part and continue to justify to themselves why they weren't approaching newcomers or following up with them. When all the glitter bags were gone— disappearing at the rate of one to two per week over several months—and none of the newcomers came back, they could pat themselves on the back for having done everything they could, expending an enormous amount of effort, and embracing a wonderful new idea. They could lament the fact that people these days just don't want to go to church, and go back to the drawing board to try and come up with another sparkly idea that would allow them to avoid the discomfort they feel when they think about approaching a newcomer. *The glitter bag is a wonderful way to avoid what is most important by ignoring what scripture tells us while simultaneously feeling as though we are doing something productive. When it doesn't work we can shift the blame outside of ourselves and our church. The glitter bag is cognitive dissonance at its finest.*

The only thing that I have found that changes this cycle is the following:

1. Name the behavior We are avoiding newcomers.
2. Recognize that fear is at the heart of it My stomach hurts when I think about it.
3. Learn realistic information What I thought would bring first-time visitors back was incorrect. My perceptions are incorrect.
4. Learn new skills I can learn how to approach newcomers in a way that will bring between 70% and 91% back.
5. Slowly replace negative *perceptions* with positive *experiences* The more I *practice* these new skills, the more I can see immediate results that negate my old perceptions.

I invite you to look deeply at how you are feeling and at the physical sensations they create. Trust that in actual practiced experience in many churches, these fears simply aren't based in reality. It is only by learning how to do this and practicing it yourself in your own church that you will begin to replace negative *perceptions* with positive *experiences*. After the first few tries, you will find that you get great *results* and build *momentum* and find yourself having *fun*. Use the prayers in this book—both for your church and before you approach a newcomer—regularly. Make room for God to calm your fears so that you can truly and warmly welcome newcomers and follow up with them.

5

APPROACHING NEWCOMERS IN AN EFFECTIVE MANNER

TIMING

*A*s discussed above, the best time to approach newcomers is at the beginning of worship. If you wait until the end, you may miss them and never get a chance to follow up with them. If they come in just before worship starts, don't be afraid to start worship a minute or two late that Sunday. The entire conversation generally takes less than sixty seconds, so that investment of one minute this Sunday has a very large chance of resulting in an actively involved member a few months from now. It is a solid investment that is worth your time.

If newcomers don't come in until after worship starts, then I catch them during the Passing of the Peace or the time when we greet one another near the beginning of worship. Either way, the script we will discuss later in this chapter is the same.

PREPARATION

Always start with the assumption that they will give you their contact information, because nineteen out of twenty will. This means that you must have a pen and something to write on in your hand when you approach them. If you use a guest book, then make sure you have the guest book with you. If you use a visitor card, make sure you have it with you. If you are just going to scribble it on a pad of paper, make sure you have the pad of paper with you.

A word about visitor cards: I used to use them all the time, but have simply switched to a pad of paper. Most of the churches I have worked with use very ineffective visitor cards. Many are small, almost business-card size, with lots of questions about whether they want to be baptized or have a visit from the minister, but with no space to write an email address. If you must use a visitor card, make it large enough to see and write on with space for actual information you need. Name first, then cell number, then email address, then physical address. Have them in this order, because if the visitor just scribbles out the first few lines, you will be able to follow up with them promptly without having to show up at their house (not recommended). Make sure that it is printed on paper stiff enough to write on, since they will likely be doing it on their laps or standing.

A word about pew pads. I generally don't advocate the use of pew pads for following up with visitors. First of all, most of the pew pads don't have enough space to write all of their contact information—especially an email address. They often have checkboxes for members, first-time visitors, out-of-towners, etc., which are superfluous. Usually everyone in the church already knows the person is a visitor, including the visitor themselves. It serves only to classify people into categories and the visitor will instantly see themselves as in an "out" category. Finally, as I mentioned earlier, if you are not willing to sit with the visitor and watch them fill out the pew pad, most visitors will only write their name, check "visitor," and leave you with nothing usable.

The method I currently use is simply a pad of paper. As the sole minister in my church, almost always preaching on a Sunday, I have a folder with a pocket inside of it where I keep my sermon notes, bulletin, and anything else I might need for the service. On the other side it holds an 8-½" x 11" pad of lined paper. I keep a pen hooked on the spine. When I approach a newcomer, I have it in my hands or tucked under my arm, closed.

If for some reason you find yourself chatting with a newcomer, but you don't have a pen or your visitor card or a pad of paper with you, then use the same script, but ask them to hold on for a moment while you grab a pen and something to write on. Then go grab them and return to collect the information immediately.

Before you approach the newcomer, pray the prayer I gave earlier. Memorize it so that you can rattle it off in your head silently while you are walking over.

Smile.

LOCATION

I generally catch people in the sanctuary because I am the minister and that is generally where I find myself when they come in. If you are an usher, you may be talking with visitors just inside the entrance to your foyer. If you are a lay leader or part of the hospitality team or a regular attendee, you may find yourself talking with them in the foyer or in the pews. I will approach people in the pews and even sit down next to them so that the conversation doesn't feel rushed. Even though it only last 60 seconds, remember that the newcomer is already overwhelmed by new sights and sounds. Approaching them in a relaxed manner and sitting down as though you have all the time in the world is important for sending the message that you care and that you are taking the time to talk with them.

THE SCRIPT

This is what I say to people when they first come in, and after many years of playing with every word, I have found this particular script to be the most effective.

[I pray the prayer listed previously as I approach. I smile.]

"Hello, is this your first time visiting?"

[They will say yes or no, usually yes.]

"Well, welcome! My name is Tracy, and I am the minister here."

[I reach out to shake their hand. They will generally respond by introducing themselves.]

"Well, welcome, it's nice to meet you. What I usually like to do when someone visits for the first time is give them a call today or tomorrow to see if they have time for a cup of coffee so that I can get to know them better and answer any questions they may have. How would you feel about that?"

[Then I wait, sometimes for a long pause. Nineteen out of twenty will say something like, "Well, sure, that sounds OK."]

"Great, let me get your phone number and email address."

[I get out my pen and paper and copy down what they tell me, making sure to show it to them to make sure I have written down what they said correctly.]

"Wonderful! I will look forward to talking with you tonight or tomorrow, and I'm glad you're here. Enjoy the service."

[I smile and stand up and go back to preparing for worship.]

Let's go through this line by line.

[I pray the prayer listed previously as I approach. I smile.]

A warm and friendly greeting works best if you are calm and happy to see them. The prayer will help with this. Smiling is important. I am assuming that you are glad that they are there and are genuinely happy to see them, but sometimes when we are nervous we forget to smile. Remember to smile!

"Hello, is this your first time visiting?"

I know that I wrote previously that using visitor identifiers— the glitter bag, the check-box on the pew pad, etc. are superfluous because in most declining churches everyone already knows that this is their first time visiting. However, the first-time visitor does not know that. If you skip this question, there are two potential problems. First, they may have visited a long time ago and you either weren't there or don't remember. If you *assume incorrectly* that they have never been there before, they may be slightly stung —however unjustifiably—that you didn't notice them, don't remember them, or don't care. I have had multiple visitors express surprise when I asked this question and then tell me long tales of how their family used to attend when they were a child and how great-grandpa and great-grandma were married in this church, or how their children came to the youth program back in 1976.

If you approached this conversation with, "I can see that you are new, here," or, "You are obviously visiting us for the first time," then they must correct your assumption, and you must back-paddle and deal with potentially hurt feelings.

If you approached this conversation with, "Is this your first time visiting?" then they can answer, "No, I've been here before," and you can respond with interest in their history with your church and a "Well, welcome back," or "Well, I'm glad to meet you," and their first experience back is a positive one.

Second, if you approach them as though you already know they are a visitor, it can increase their feelings of being an outsider, as everyone so clearly knows one another at your church that the visitor is quickly identified as an anomaly. It can also project a feeling of desperation on your part that your church is so small and desperate for visitors that you latch onto them. This is a common mistake churches make, and it can be either subtle or overt.

[They will say yes or no, usually yes.] "Well, welcome! My name is Tracy, and I am the minister here."

I say, "Well, welcome!" *after* they identify themselves as a visitor. This is important for exactly the reasons listed above. I introduce myself and then give my role, but I do not introduce myself with a fancy title. Different churches have their own ways of addressing their ministers, but I caution you against introducing yourselves as "Holy Reverend Father Richard McGillicuddy the Third." As the minister, I am usually already wearing my robe and stole when I approach them, so I don't need a big fancy title to clarify my role. A big fancy title is also a lot to digest and they may fear that they will repeat it back to you incorrectly. The same goes for lay leaders. "Hi, I'm Nancy and I'm part of our welcome team," is better than, "Hi, I'm Mrs. Nancy Peabody, the Chair of the Board of Trustees and the Secretary of the Hospitality and Outreach Committees."

[I reach out to shake their hand. They will generally respond by introducing themselves.]

If they don't come forth with their name at this point, I ask, "What is your name?" Be aware that they may be overwhelmed with the new experience, and may falter briefly on basic social conversation. Don't take it personally, just ask for their name and shake their hand.

"Well it's nice to meet you. What I usually like to do when someone visits for the first time is give them a call today or tomorrow to see if they have time for a cup of coffee so that I can get to know them better and answer any questions they may have."

This part is the meat of the script, because it explains to them exactly what is going to happen *before* we ever get to talking about contact information. This is deliberate, because if you ask for contact information before you explain what you are going to do with it, they will stop listening to you while they think about whether they want to give it. Without the information you need to give them, they will likely have a negative response because they don't yet know what you are going to do with the information.

Be aware that I don't use the word *you*. I don't say, "What I would like to do since you are visiting for the first time is give *you* a call to see if *you* have time for a cup of coffee so that I can get to know *you* better." The reason for the difference is this: If I tell them what I would like to do with *them specifically*, it can put them on the defensive in a subtle way. I very intentionally give them this information in the third person and use the word *usually* because it conveys to them that this is a very common occurrence.

Be aware that I don't use the words *newcomer* or *first-time visitor*, as these are labels that designate them as an anomaly and different from a *member*. Instead, I say, "When someone visits for the first time..." which describes a human being taking a particular action.

Notice that I tell them exactly what will happen next. "I give them a call today or tomorrow to see if they have time for a cup of coffee." This is about integrity. I am telling them right up front exactly what will happen, what *usually* happens. Right here in this very first conversation, we are starting to demonstrate that at this church, we are up front about our intentions, and that our words match our actions. If in your church you have a different follow-up, then be clear about that. I tell them that I will call them today or tomorrow because that keeps the follow-up within the first 24 hours, which increases the likelihood that they will return. I choose coffee because coffee implies *warm, but informal*. It is also versatile. Coffee can be had at a local café, at my office, or—only if they suggest it—in their home. If in your church your minister or other designated follow-up person *usually* gives people who visit for the first time a call Monday afternoon to see if they can come to the office to have tea and biscuits, then tell them that. If you don't know what the plan at your church is, then ask the minister or yourself or whoever will be doing the follow-up what the plan is. If they don't have one, then ask whether they can give the newcomer a call within 24 hours to arrange a meeting over coffee, and use that plan. Just make sure that whatever it is you are going to do, you are completely honest about it *before* you ask for their contact information.

I would strongly discourage inviting them to have a beer or wine or any other form of alcohol, as that means that either you will be meeting in a bar or drinking alcohol alone in your office or in their home. This implies a date, and this is not the intention of the first meeting. It could also get you into serious legal trouble! Some churches are starting ministries in breweries with titles like "Theology on Tap," and such, and those can bring some lively discussion to some previously unexplored areas, but it should not be the arena for your first meeting with a newcomer.

The phrase, "...so that I can get to know them better and answer any questions they may have," states your intentions. This is your true purpose, so state it clearly so that they have no misunderstandings about why you may be calling them to see if they have time for coffee. You are not going to ask them whether they have accepted Jesus as their own personal savior. You are not going to proposition them. You are not going to try to read harsh passages from the Bible to them. You are not going to demand to know whether they have been baptized. You are not going to stage an intervention with a team of people. You are being very clear that you want to *get to know them better* and *answer any questions they may have.* Meeting over a cup of coffee is conducive to this because it is a quiet activity that invites conversation and it suggests a level of informality that doesn't feel like an interview. Later in this book, we will be going over how to have the conversation over coffee, and I promise you that all of the questions you ask will be geared toward *getting to know them better* and *answering any questions they may have.* What we are thinking, what we are saying, and what we are doing are all in alignment. We are demonstrating that we have integrity, honorable intentions, and healthy boundaries right from the beginning, and this is important.

"How would you feel about that?"

Be aware that I am not asking them, "So what do you think, can I get your number?" This is a yes-or-no, black-or-white question that locks them into one of two finite positions. In fact, I am not asking them for their contact information at all. I am asking them how they would feel about receiving a phone call today or tomorrow to see if they have time for a cup of coffee so that I can get to know them better and answer any questions they may have. This is critical, because when they say that would feel all right— and nineteen out of twenty do—they are already feeling good about having coffee and letting me get to know them better. When I call that night or the next day, all we have to do is arrange a time and place because they are already feeling positive about meeting over coffee and are thinking about what questions they may have and how they are feeling cared for, because 1) someone called them back and 2) someone is taking the time to get to know them.

If I ask them for their contact information but don't tell them what I am going to do with it, when I call them to invite them for coffee, they often find the call jarring, because they weren't expecting it, and they have to decide whether to say yes or no while they are feeling a little caught off guard. By explaining exactly what we are going to do and then asking them how they feel about it, when they say they feel alright about it, then they are looking forward to your call and to your invitation and to the meeting. When you follow through and do what you said you were going to do, they see it as confirmation of what they were already sensing—that your church is a safe place that honors boundaries and has integrity. These feelings are much more conducive to fruitful conversation than feeling thrown off guard because they got a jarring phone call they weren't expecting.

[Then I WAIT, sometimes for a long pause. Nineteen out of twenty will say something like, "Well, sure, that sounds OK."]

Be aware that newcomers may have a prolonged pause as they think about what you just said. Remember, this is a new place for them, and they are—whether you realize it or not—on sensory overload. They are seeing new sights and new people, sensing new smells and hearing new sounds, and now a person they have never met before just gave them an enormous amount of infor- mation. Even though you've only said three sentences to them, you have given them your name and your role, told them what may happen in the next twenty-four hours, expressed an implied invitation to have coffee, and stated your intentions to get to know them better and answer any questions they may have. Most noticeably, you are doing all of this just as worship is about to start. To top it all off, you just asked them to think about how they feel about *all* of this and then to express those feelings in words. It will take them several moments to process all of this and come back to you with a response. Be prepared for a pregnant—though not uncomfortable—pause.

The worst thing you can do at this moment—and the thing that most people do the first time they approach a newcomer—is get a case of diarrhea of the mouth. They notice that the newcomer is pausing, fear that perhaps the newcomer is skeptical, and start trying to reassure them by saying things like, "only if you feel like it," or "no pressure if you don't want to," or "I want to assure you that we won't spam you or put your information into a database without your permission," or "I don't want you to think that I'm pushy," or any number of other disclaimers that give the newcomer some reason to feel your tension, mistrust you, and back out, instead of thinking about how they feel about your stated *intentions* and *next steps*.

So *wait*. Smile, sit there calmly, and keep your mouth shut until they answer.

If they say "no," remember to say, "Thank you for telling me, that's why we ask. I sure hope you'll come back again soon so that we can get to know you better." If they say "yes," then the next logical step is to collect their contact information.

6

THE FOLLOW-UP PHONE CALL

*T*his is the script that I use when I follow up with people. I call them first on their phone, because that is more personal than sending an email. However, I find that most people do not pick up when I call, and it goes to their voicemail, forcing me to leave a message. This is likely because even though I introduced myself, they might not make the immediate connection between my first and last name as it shows up on their caller ID, and "Tracy the minister" or "Pastor Tracy," as I introduced myself in the church. Generally, it is only women in their 80s or 90s who pick up their phones, because they only have house lines. In general, the younger-than-80 generation prefers to text or email rather than talk on the phone. That is just fine. They can respond in whichever way they prefer, but I will reach out in a personal manner regardless.

The good news is that since you are talking on the phone, and since you are usually going to find yourself leaving a voicemail message, you can read this script rather than having to memorize it.

Hello! This is _____ from _____ Church.

I hope you are doing well! I wanted to tell you again how much I enjoyed meeting you on Sunday and see when you might have time for a cup of coffee so that I can get to know you better and answer any questions you may have.

I have time _____, _____, and _____.

Please let me know what will work best for you.

My phone number is _____. (This is my cell phone and the best way to get hold of me. You can call or text.)

I also have your email address, so I will send you an email with the same information and you can respond whichever way is most convenient.

I'll look forward to hearing from you!

Then I send an email with exactly the same information. Most of the time, I will get an email or a text message in response telling me when they are free.

People often ask me how I choose a location for the meeting. This usually happens when the newcomer responds with the time that works best for them, and they will ask, "Where do you want to meet?" This is a situation that must be delicately handled because there is so much skepticism over churches and ministers these days. You don't want to push for a meeting at your office because that might feel too isolated and private for their comfort level. At the same time, they may have a big issue on their heart they may not feel comfortable discussing in a public location like a café. I never suggest coming to their house, because this generation may feel that this is a bit invasive, but ladies in their 80s usually ask me to come over for tea because they enjoy hosting, are familiar with the older tradition of having a minister come to the house, and generally don't drive or don't enjoy driving anymore. This is how I usually address this issue:

"Is there a coffee place near you that you like to go to?" If they are new in town or don't know any coffee places, they will say so and I will suggest one that I know near the church that is conducive to conversation. If they are not new in town, they generally suggest a place near them that is familiar. We always pay for the coffee. I rarely take someone to lunch except in the rare case in which they are only free on their lunch hour. The coffee meeting takes a minimum of an hour, so make sure to plan accordingly. I rarely plan coffee meetings immediately before something else, just in case they run long.

Be aware that sometimes people are really busy and will schedule a meeting with you two or even three weeks out. This is totally normal, and they will often continue coming to worship services until you can meet, because you followed up with them in a personal manner within twenty-four hours.

Every once in a while, there will be someone who doesn't return my call. It happens. There are very rarely people who feel OK about a coffee meeting when you ask them, but then change their mind and tell you no later, or simply don't respond to your follow-up. In these cases, I generally reach out about three times over two weeks, and then let it go.

But in most cases, people will be eager to meet you over coffee, respond to your call, and arrange for a meeting within two weeks.

SEVEN POINTS OF CONTACT

*O*nce you have set the meeting for a cup of coffee, you must widen your focus –from simply getting their contact information so that you can follow up with them and have them come back again—to your long-term goal, which is getting them fully involved in the church and considering membership. At this point, I should clarify why I advocate having coffee meetings with newcomers, versus having a personal follow-up that is simply sending them a hand-written card, letter, or personal card telling them again how much you enjoyed meeting them and welcoming them, or a loaf of bread/basket of cookies/apple pie on the doorstep. These are personal follow-ups and the research tells us that they will get people to return at a rate of about 70%. However, our goal is not simply to get people to return for one more Sunday. Our goal is to grow our church, which means that we want people to become actively involved and seriously considering membership. In order to do this, we must do several things.

First of all, research tells us that newcomers to a church must establish seven points of contact within the first three to six months in order to seriously consider membership. If they do not have these established, they will not be interested in membership and will likely fade away from the church after a few months. If, on the other hand, they have seven points of contact established, they will likely stay actively involved in the church and seriously consider membership, whether or not they ever actually formally join.

In my experience these seven points of contact are not only critical in order for attendees to seriously consider membership, but they are important to sustain the longevity of the attendee's membership and the health of the church. As I have watched churches go through conflict, in my experience it is the ones who have *fewer* points of contact who threaten to leave when something happens that they don't like, or when conflict arises within the congregation. On the other hand, members who have *more* points of contact may be opinionated, may be passionate, and may be vocal, but are much less likely to threaten to leave, as they are heavily invested in the church and its vitality.

Points of contact are ways in which members are connected to the church. Here are some examples of points of contact:

1. They enjoy attending worship service regularly.
2. They are receiving pastoral care from the minister.
3. They or their spouse enjoys singing in choir.
4. Their young children love attending Sunday school.
5. Their teenagers love attending youth group.
6. They or their spouse enjoy serving at the church's food pantry, or cooking for the meal that the church serves regularly at the local homeless shelter, or in any other hands-on, service-oriented ministry.
7. They enjoy donating money to the church or to its specific ministries, including the Pastor's Discretionary Fund.
8. They enjoy visiting the house-bound.
9. They or their spouse or children have made a friend

within the congregation and they enjoy a common activity outside of church.

Generally speaking, we don't count exactly the number of points of contact for anybody, as it is nearly impossible to do. However, as ministers we can be instrumental in facilitating the first three or four points of contact. The coffee meeting is an ideal place to do that.

In my experience, most people come to church for a reason. Nobody ever gets up on a Sunday and just decides to go to a new church that day because they are bored. If people are bored on a Sunday morning, there are dozens of other, much more entertaining activities that people could engage in besides going to church. If people come to church, it is because of two very specific and compelling reasons:

1. They have a spiritual need that must be met, be it a longing, a wound, an emptiness, a deep question, a crisis of faith, a desire for their children's faith development, etc.
2. They have a deep desire to give back, to make a difference in the world by expressing their gifts in a community of faith that has integrity and practices what Jesus practiced and preached.

By sending a personal card or dropping a goodie bag on their doorstep, you are definitely sending a clear message that you care, and that should not be discounted. It is very likely (70% likely) to effect their return the following Sunday and possibly one or two after that. But our goal is not only to get them to fill our pews, but to have them actively involved in the church so that we can meet their spiritual needs and facilitate their desire to serve their community, using their gifts with integrity. This requires taking the time to get to know them so that you can understand their spiritual needs, gifts and desires. Dropping a goodie bag on the doorstep is thoughtful, but not conducive to this level of conversation. Sending a welcome is personal, but not conducive to this level of conversation. Calling them up to briefly welcome them is conducive to beginning this conversation, but stops short of it.

On the other hand, breaking bread together is absolutely conducive to this level of conversation. Even if it is just drinking a cup of coffee and a pastry, it forces us to sit down together, look each other in the eye, and see within each other both our humanity and our divinity. By sitting across a table from each other, we are (whether we state it overtly or not) engaging in an ancient ritual that has brought people together to sit as equals for millennia, and it is something that Jesus practiced regularly for exactly these reasons. As I have spent many years and countless hours sitting down with first-time visitors to churches, I have found that there are ways to have superficial conversations and ways to get to the heart of who they are, their deepest spiritual needs, their greatest gifts, and their deepest desires to serve. When we do this right from the outset, we can begin facilitating their participation in the church, their seven points of contact, and their investment in the community right from the very first meeting. As a result, the newcomer thrives and the church thrives.

8

THE FOUR BIG QUESTIONS

*W*hen I meet with a person who has visited the church for the first time, I schedule an hour on my calendar, and try not to schedule anything immediately following. When two people sit down to break bread together and have deep conversation about spiritual needs, gifts, and our deepest desires, you never know how the Holy Spirit will move, so I try not to plan my day in a way that might cut that short. Keep in mind also that many people have never had the luxury of an entire hour of a minister's time, especially one who is genuinely interested in getting to know them better as a child of God. As the conversation progresses, it may open them up in ways that neither of you were expecting.

When you meet, it is natural to start with get-to-know-you questions, like how their day is going, what they do for a living, where they've just moved from, whether or not they have a partner, children, what they are studying, etc. After the first several minutes of superficial questions of this sort, you will sense a lull in the conversation. At this point, I ask my first Big Question.

SO, DID YOU GROW UP IN THE CHURCH?

This question speaks to one of the primary reasons that they are coming to church, the fact that they have a deep spiritual need. But the reality is that if you asked them, "What spiritual needs brought you to our church?" you would likely be met with confused silence. Likewise, if you asked them to lay back on a couch and start at the beginning and share their entire spiritual journey from the day they were born until the present moment, being sure to detail any major traumas, setbacks, or disappointments, you would be met with stony silence because they don't know you or trust you well enough to be that vulnerable. But by asking this question phrased in this manner, they must think back to their childhood church or their childhood lack of church, which, except in really rare cases, is not your church, because of course they have only just visited it for the first time a week or so ago.

As they begin to answer this question, you will be amazed to hear how they link that experience so many years ago to how they ended up walking through your doors. You will hear each church or denomination that they attended, what their experience was, why they were there, why they left, and how they ended up coming to you. You will often hear that partings from previous churches were not healthy, peaceful, positive, or loving. They will often allude to—or detail outright—church dysfunction and/or clergy abuses. People have told me of being physically assaulted because they were gay. I have heard numerous stories of leaving churches because their mothers were shunned after divorcing abusive husbands. People have told me of sudden partings because their spouses died and they were too old to live alone, so they uprooted and moved across the country to live with family. People have told me of clergy sexually abusing children or women, and leaving when the church covered it up. People have told me of leaving in disgust when churches went into conflict over whether to fire a pastor. People have shared deep wounds of when they left their lifelong church community because their church wouldn't accept or ordain or marry gays or lesbians, women, or transgendered individuals. People have told me of leaving when churches refused to baptize their children. People have told me of leaving because, after the Westboro Baptist Church picketed the church, the lay leaders shunned those whom the WBC had targeted. As you listen to these stories, do not undervalue either the enormous amount of emotional trouble they went to in order to find your church, or the incredible opportunity you are being given.

For those who were not raised in a church, I have heard heart-wrenching stories of being raised with intense skepticism of anything religious. People have told me of going through many of life's most sacred rites of passage or transformational experiences —puberty, leaving home, marriage, death of a loved one, divorce, childbirth, alcoholism, drug abuse, child abuse, miscarriage, widowhood, extreme poverty, hunger, homelessness, coming to the country as a refugee—without any ritual, counseling, framing, guidance, prayer, or any understanding of God's love for them. They have told me of deep longing, of constant seeking, only to bump into exploitative Christian churches, abusive religious practices, or Christian ministers whose faith and understanding were superficial, angry, and repetitive. As above, as you listen to these stories, do not undervalue either the uphill battle they have endured to find your church, or the sacred possibilities you are being given.

Prepare yourself to hear a lengthy and painful story when you ask this question, and then when it happens, say a prayer of gratitude for it. We say a prayer of gratitude because it is a gift for so many reasons. First of all, it means that the person trusts you enough to tell you, which means that you are building a real relationship on a meaningful level. Second, recognize that this may be the first time this person has had a chance to tell this whole story to anyone who would listen and care. So they are casting their burden, which shows a leap of faith. Third, understand that this gives you valuable insight into what this person values, where their passions lie, and what they will and will not tolerate in a church. Fourth, recognize that despite all of their pain, all of their emotional baggage, all of their past negative experiences, they took a chance on church again and picked your church to give them a reason to have faith again. Finally, be cognizant of the fact that this is a sacred opportunity both to facilitate personal healing for the newcomer, and also to rebuild the integrity of the church universal. This is a time to be the best minister that God has called you to be.

When people tell me terrible things that churches have done to them, I do two things. First, I treat it as though a person is revealing a trauma that has happened, because if they have never processed these situations and never received any closure, the wounds will still be fresh, no matter how much time has passed. When the person is all done telling their story, when they finally get to why they are looking for you, the first thing I say is "Thank you." Then I acknowledge the courage it took to share their experience and I acknowledge its impact. I almost always apologize on behalf of the church. This is what I usually say:

"Wow, that's huge. Thank you for telling me. I want to acknowledge how much guts it took for you to tell me all of that. That church really screwed up, and they were wrong. On behalf of the church, I want to apologize to you. That is not what God's love is supposed to look like. I want to assure you that I would not allow that to happen in this church. If it ever does, I want you to let me know immediately so that I can put a stop to it."

I cannot express to you how much of a difference this makes to people. Oftentimes when churches behave badly, a person's concerns are dismissed, minimized, or hushed. Sometimes when they speak up they are targeted. Oftentimes in these conversations, this is the first time that their experience has been acknowledged as impactful, difficult, and wrong, let alone apologized. But if we are to be individuals and churches with integrity, these abuses must be acknowledged and these apologies must be made. It is the only way that true healing can begin.

You may wonder why I would make apologies on behalf of someone I never met for an abuse that I never perpetrated. If we truly believe that we are the Body of Christ, then when one person causes damage, we all suffer. We all suffer the pain that was caused, and we all suffer the guilt that is borne. If we all strive for the forgiveness of guilt and the healing that must occur, then we all must take responsibility for the action, make the apology, and ensure that it never happens again.

At the core of this is the integrity of our beliefs. In this statement, we not only acknowledge the wrong and try to make it right, but we also clearly delineate what God's love is and what it is not. "That is not what God's love is supposed to look like," begins to recapture what church is supposed to be and where we have failed. It also indicates a lack of integrity between what people believe, what they say they believe, and how they act out their beliefs. It also opens up a small window for hope in new possibilities for the newcomer by re-equating the church with God's love, *when actions and words are in alignment with the beliefs about Beloved Community.*

Oftentimes newcomers will tell me of abuses and dysfunction that they saw perpetrated toward and among people around them. Sometimes they will tell me of abuses that were perpetrated toward them directly. In my experience, this most often occurs with members of the LGBT community. Once I acknowledge that what they suffered was indeed a wrong, an abuse, a discrimination, or an exploitation *without minimizing it*, we may have to go one step further by beginning to undo the damage that was done. For example, people will often ask if it is true that they are an abomination, or that they are going to hell, or whether particularly judgmental biblical passages are true. I often respond by reminding them that *the Bible says clearly that they were created in the image of God and that they are good.* I am continually surprised by how many people have never heard that, have never been taught that.

This question, *"So, did you grow up in the church,"* has led to more healing, more forgiveness, more health, and more honesty than any other question. The more I ask this question, the more I see what an integrity problem we have in churches today, and the more I have an opportunity to restore it. With this question I am able to get to the heart of where people are at spiritually and where they want to be. Most importantly, I am able to begin building genuine relationship with the newcomer.

WHAT BRINGS YOU THE GREATEST JOY?

This is a question that sometimes feels a little out of place. It is not something that people generally use in casual conversation, such as, "What did you do this weekend?" or "How's it going?" So I often preface it with, "This is a question I always like to ask people when I am getting to know them…" It gives them a heads-up that we are changing directions and makes the transition less jarring. Whenever I ask this question, I get a very long and thoughtful pause. People have rarely been asked this before. Have you ever been asked this question before? Probably not! Yet it is such a vital question for many reasons. First of all, when people finally answer they will usually be sharing their passion with you, their gift. Second, their passion and gift usually translate very well into a ministry within the church. As I said earlier, people generally come to church for two main reasons—they have a deep spiritual need that they are trying to meet, and they genuinely want to serve—to make a lasting and positive difference in the world. Whatever brings them the greatest joy can usually be channeled to make a lasting and positive difference in the world through the church.

People will often speak of their love for music or singing or art. People will often speak of their love of working with their hands to build or create things. People will often speak of spending time with their families and especially their grandchildren. People will often speak of finding joy in helping people who are less fortunate. I have never, ever, ever, even once, had anyone ever tell me that their greatest joy lies in exploiting people, enacting violence, amassing as much wealth as possible, or hoarding luxuries. If you ask this question, don't be surprised if what brings them the greatest joy translates directly into an existing ministry within the church, or into a ministry that your church could start.

At one church where I served, our music during Sunday worship was lacking. We were trying to implement more contemporary and upbeat music but with just a piano and a choir we needed something with a little more oomph. I noticed we had a drum set in our basement, but there was no one who attended who could play the drums, and no one knew anyone who knew anyone who could. I was talking with a newcomer over coffee and asked him what brought him the greatest joy. He thought for a long minute and then said, "Playing drums in a praise band!"

One time I served a church where the Sunday school teachers were burning out and fresh ideas were few and far between. I asked a newcomer what brought him the greatest joy, and he said, "My job. I am a puppeteer. I love building puppets and creating puppet shows."

At one church where the population was aging, we had been struggling for almost a year to find ways to support our graying population. We had held seminars on Wills and Trusts and End-of-Life Decisions, brought in pharmacists and nurses to help people keep track of their medications, and so on. I asked a newcomer this question and he said, "I find the greatest joy in my second career. I absolutely love teaching yoga to people above the age of 50 because it is such a great form of low-impact exercise for both the mind and the body."

At one church we launched a Homework Club for low-income students whose parents don't speak English as a first language. Over several months different students showed me stories they were writing for fun. As our afterschool program turned into a summer school program, multiple middle school girls expressed an interest in creative writing classes. When I asked a newcomer this question around that time, he spoke passionately about his lifelong desire to write, his volunteer work with kids at the local library, and how he had late in life finally become a published author of multiple fictional novels. He asked if we could use any more volunteers at the Homework Club he had heard about. He became a creative writing teacher for after-school classes and summer classes for these youth, published their works, and took them on field trips to writing centers. The whole program blossomed.

What is important to note is that in some cases people's careers do translate well into ministry. However, I do not ask them what they do for a living and then ask them to translate their career skills and expertise into a ministry, because a person's career is not necessarily what brings them the greatest joy. I have heard of many cases of churches who try and convince the school teachers in their congregation to teach Sunday school because they have so many skills in that area, or accountants to serve as the church treasurer, construction workers to serve on the maintenance crew. What I have found, however, is that school teachers rarely want to do this because their jobs are so demanding that on Sunday they need peace and a chance to restore their spiritual batteries. The same is true for many, many people who work during the week. Even though they may be good at their jobs, even though they may be successful at their jobs, even though they may enjoy their jobs, that doesn't mean that their jobs bring them great joy or are indicative of their gifts for ministry.

However, facilitating a person's ability to express their greatest joy in a meaningful way that makes a difference in the world benefits the newcomer, the church, and the community at large. It also reduces the likelihood of burnout and stress. By asking what brings people the greatest joy, you can find a much better—more positive, healthy, joyful, and passionate—fit for them as they seek to serve through the church.

When I ask this question and learn more about what brings an individual the greatest joy, I then try to facilitate their entry into service and participation. I will identify the ministry or ministries that I think might be a good extension of their passion and ask them if they are interested in checking it out. If they are at all interested, I use a model of invitation very similar to when I first told them I would call them and ask them if they have time for a cup of coffee. *I do not* refer them to our website. *I do not* simply give them the time and encourage them to check it out. *I do not* give them a flier (with or without a glittery bag) and hope that they will follow up and come back.

If I give them the information and expect them to follow up on their own, then I have plunked them right back into the same situation they were in before they came to church the first time. They have to find the location, show up at just the right time, worry about what to wear, and then walk into a room full of people they have not met before. In this form, the situation is unnecessarily daunting and uncomfortable for a first-time visitor.

Instead, I say something like the following:

"Leticia Brown is our music director and the person who leads our choir rehearsals. I would like to give Leticia your contact information so that she can call you and give you more information about the program and the next upcoming event. How would you feel about that?"

I cannot recall a single instance in which a first-time visitor has felt uncomfortable with that. Most of the time, they appear relieved. Immediately following the meeting, I send an email to the head of the ministry that says:

"A newcomer has expressed interest in singing in the choir/serving at the food pantry/bringing refreshments for the coffee hour/serving as liturgist during worship/etc. Would you please give her a call, tell her about the program, and personally invite her to the next event? Here is her contact information..."

By having the head of the ministry contact the newcomer, it takes the pressure off. It also begins to acclimate them to the ministry so that when they get there they know what to expect, feel invited (not invasive) and already know someone who will be there. If the head of the program calls them, they can give them a heads-up on little details that make an enormous difference in a person's positive experience—i.e. parking is free if you go around to the other side of the block; it's an unwritten rule that everyone brings finger foods to share; it's chilly in that room so people generally get there ten minutes early to get a seat near the heater; you'll want to bring a notepad and pen to take notes; you'll want to wear heavy-duty shoes because there are a lot of narrow stair-cases; this particular meeting everyone is supposed to bring a white elephant gift; the head of the ministry will be in the office on the left so come find them when you arrive so they can show you around and introduce you, etc.

By going to this extra amount of trouble, you are going a long way toward *welcoming the stranger*. You are ensuring that they will have the best possible chance of actually experiencing that joy when they express their gifts in this new ministry. You are increasing the chances that they will attend and return.

SO WHAT DID YOU THINK OF WORSHIP ON SUNDAY?

With this question, timing is everything. If I were to ask this question when we first sit down, I would likely get a pat response such as a superficial question or the dreaded—and meaningless—"it was fine." However, by this point in the conversation a lot has already been accomplished. We have moved far beyond the superficial stuff. The newcomer has talked in detail about their spiritual journey and what brings them the greatest joy. They have addressed important issues and found a healing response with integrity. They are most likely already invested in returning to the church because they are planning on trying out a ministry and are looking forward to getting a phone call from its leader. Trust has been established and they are talking with a minister as a minister. So at this point when we ask, "So, what did you think of worship on Sunday?" the answer will be much more honest, and so much richer.

The responses to this question can go in any direction. People will often have questions about aspects of the liturgy, especially if something was unfamiliar. People may have probing questions about the sermon, or share how it affected them. People may ask about certain items in the sanctuary, such as artwork.

Oftentimes, people will tell you something that made them uncomfortable. This is incredibly valuable because sometimes we lose perspective of our liturgy, traditions, and church culture. A person with a fresh pair of eyes that is willing to tell you honestly what they experienced can be very eye-opening and alert you to things that may need to be dealt with.

I once took a youth group to a neighboring church for their 125th-anniversary service and celebration. None of us could fully participate because there were no hymnals and none of the songs were printed. It was just assumed that everyone knew all the words to all the songs. I met with the minister (who I already knew) later and they were shocked to find that newcomers experienced that confusion. In the church where something went noticeably wrong in every service, it was only because of the newcomers that I realized that was a blessing and learned not to fret and cringe (internally) so much. It was a newcomer who once explained to me how wonky the collection was—with the way the minister faced during the service, I had never seen it. After this heads-up, I made a point of watching the following Sunday. It was definitely a convoluted and discombobulated three-minute period of acrobatics and aerobics with plate-passing switcheroos that could have been a circus act. It turns out it was a holdover from a six-plate system used when the church was much larger. My observations led to some major discussions and changes around sanctuary layout and how to restructure the way the ushers collected.

It was a twenty-something newcomer that let me know they never carried cash or a checkbook, and asked how they could donate electronically so they didn't feel so uncomfortable being unable to participate when the plates were passed. This led to the implementation of an electronic giving system. They may tell you that a member was overly aggressive in hugging during the greeting time, or said something inappropriate to them.

At one point a church hired me as a consultant but asked me to come incognito one Sunday because they couldn't figure out why newcomers never came back. I came with my children and it happened to be Mother's Day. Not one person greeted me and the ushers clearly saw me but neither smiled nor approached. They expected people to find the table near the entrance on their own and help themselves to a program. I had no idea whether there was Sunday school or whether children generally stayed in the sanctuary. It wasn't until I had been seated with my children for more than five minutes that one very friendly woman came over to say hello and spontaneously offered me a flower from a bouquet she had brought because it was Mother's Day and I had children with me. In the consulting session after the worship service I told them of my experience and told them point-blank that they should switch their ushers and replace them with the woman who had given me the flower. They were shocked because until that point they hadn't known this was happening.

A newcomer once told me that she was concerned because the

children started in the sanctuary, but then left to go to Sunday school after the Children's Moment during worship. After service, she had no idea where her children were or how to collect them and she had several frantic minutes wondering where to go and who to ask.

Newcomers will often tell you something that is important to them—positive or negative—about the worship service. They may tell you how much they enjoyed the music, the candles, or the form of prayer. They may tell you about which member was most friendly and/or helpful to them. You may find that some members' names come up again and again as being especially warm and friendly. This should inform you as to who may make a good greeter or even someone to follow up with newcomers over coffee in the future. Newcomers will also often express—straight out—their desire to help with some aspect of worship service. If you can facilitate this, they will have found another point of contact and another way to express their gifts and joy.

This question will help you to see your church with fresh eyes, tackle issues before they do damage, recognize positive people and/or experiences in your church, and better understand what is important to your newcomer. Whatever the newcomer tells you, if it is honest it will be valuable.

DID YOU HAVE ANY OTHER QUESTIONS BEFORE WE GO?

As in the previous example, timing is everything. If you started the conversation with, "So did you have any questions for me?" you would likely get superficial questions, or a very insincere "Not really..." But at this point you have built the solid foundations of trust, relationship, and sacred sharing. They know that they can share—and have already shared— things with you of a deep and personal nature and you will respond with a healthy and gentle pastoral presence. This time has been extremely valuable to them.

Many times people will have nothing more to ask. They have shared and gained valuable information and they will simply respond, "No, I think you've answered all my questions and I'm looking forward to seeing you all next Sunday."

Oftentimes, however, if there is anything that has been bubbling under the surface, it will often come forth at this point. I often refer to it as people dropping a bomb, because often whatever they say next is big, is disturbing, and they have usually been waiting for years to find a safe place to say it. I have had people come out of the closet to me at this point in the conversation. I have had people ask me whether it's true that women have to be silent and wear veils in the church. I have had people ask me whether evolution or dinosaurs are real. One individual took a big breath and said, "I am gay and have been living with another man for the past two years. My family lives in Russia and doesn't know. They are coming to visit me next week. What should I do?" Once a young woman said, "I wasn't sure whether I should bring this up, but a few years ago I told my family I was gay, my family forced me into gay conversion therapy, and I don't know whether that was OK to do to me." One first-time visitor asked me whether it was true that Eve—and women in general—were really the root of all evil. One man asked me whether I'd be willing to talk some sense into his wife. She had not attended church since she was a teenager, but had in recent years begun exploring Buddhist practices such as meditation, and wore prayer beads that just happened to have some "pagan" symbols. He fearfully—and misguidedly—believed that these were signs she was practicing Satanism. I've had a couple ask me whether the husband should get baptized again, since his other two baptisms didn't really count—the first was when he was just a baby and the second was "coerced" when he wanted to marry a Catholic and they said he wasn't allowed to unless he was baptized again as a Catholic. I've had multiple people ask me about the validity of passages in Leviticus, usually but not always the ones about men laying with men. One woman asked me whether the church could help with her electric bill—she had reached the point of turning off the circuit breaker to her heater in the middle of December and simply couldn't afford her bill anymore. There are not enough pages to detail the enormous number and complicated nature of the circumstances that led to this situation for herself, her husband and her young child.

At least six different times, newcomers have asked me whether demon possession is real. This question has come up so many times that I now incorporate it into the workshops that I teach, and so I will devote some time to discussing it here. If this question comes up, I have learned to move the conversation to a more private place where it cannot be easily overheard. We may move to a quieter table in the café, or take a walk outside to continue it. Then, this is what I usually say: "I'm not 100% sure. But what I do know is that if it is real, it doesn't happen randomly. People don't just wander down the street drinking their latte and suddenly find that they are possessed by an evil spirit. However, it is very common for people who have been sexually assaulted as children and who have never really processed or healed from that experience to believe that there is an evil spirit or force inhabiting their body, their room, or their home. That's because a child's mind can't process what is happening to them at the time, so they turn it into a metaphor for a force that is bigger and stronger than them, and that intends to harm them, and this can carry through to adulthood, when they simply fear that they are under threat of possession by a demon or evil spirit. What do you think about that?" Every single time, they have responded by telling me about the sexual harm that was done to them years ago.

In each of these conversations, newcomers' questions had enormous and life-changing implications. Obviously they required a much bigger conversation than a simple yes-or-no answer. Often, they led to recommendations for counseling, professional help, and more than once, police involvement. Very often, these questions led to an impromptu Bible study. Many times, these people had never found a safe or informed place to ask their question. Often, they had waited years or even decades for that safe place to appear. Without taking the time to talk with them, build trust, and embody integrity, they may never have found that safe place.

When we get to this point in the conversation, we are in a sacred place. We have our finger on the pulse of Christianity. We are at a convergence of being our most vulnerable, loving unconditionally, being our most pastoral, and doing real work in healing, forgiveness, study of scripture, reconciliation, and giving sanctuary. In these moments when we honor their experience, facilitate their healing, and pledge to walk with them on their journey, we are doing the real work that Jesus calls us to do. At this point, the conversation stops being about growing the church, and it evolves into making disciples and building God's kingdom. It transforms both the newcomer and the minister.

CLOSING

As you are parting, this is an appropriate time to ask whether they would like to be put onto the newsletter mailing or email list, confirm that you have their complete contact information, get their physical address if you don't already have it, and reiterate any plans you have made to put them into contact with lay leaders, professionals, or other resources. Make sure to thank them for taking the time, and tell them you'll look forward to seeing them soon.

9

FREQUENTLY ASKED QUESTIONS

Usually at the end of workshops I open the floor to questions. Here are some of the most common.

"BUT MONDAY IS THE PASTOR'S DAY OFF!"

People—ministers especially—always worry that Monday is the minister's day off. They ask how ministers are logistically supposed to call first-time visitors within 24 hours when they take Monday off. There are three options here:

First of all, calling one, two, or even three newcomers will take less than ten minutes. Most of the time the call goes straight to voicemail and all you have to do is leave a message. If you follow up with an email, add another five minutes, knowing that you can copy-paste the suggested email in this book and just change the times you are available. In the wildest scenario, if you had five newcomers on a single Sunday, you might have to spend all of twenty minutes following up. Expect to get emails and text messages back over the next day or so in order to set the date and the time of the coffee meeting. Yes, technically, these twenty minutes of work fall on a Sunday evening or a Monday which is—

strictly speaking—during the minister's time off. At the same time, ministers' schedules are fluid, and this one small investment in time will pay enormous dividends.

Second, I switched my day off years ago. I followed the excellent example of my former minister and take Fridays and Saturdays off. Monday is a difficult day because all of the activities on Sunday are indeed emotionally and physically exhausting. So I do my best to work from home on Monday and keep my meetings light that day so I can focus more on organization, correspondence, and writing. But I found that switching my days off to Friday and Saturday makes my work week much more productive, and newcomer follow-up much more fruitful. Ministers may want to consider changing their traditional schedule in order focus on this important work.

Third, congregations may need to step in in multiple ways. Congregations can step up by urging the minister to prioritize this work over all other work and supporting them in doing so. For example, is the minister unable to follow up Sunday evening because they are in meetings after church and teaching Bible study in the evenings? Lay leadership can step in to take over these duties so that the minister can spend time following up with newcomers. It is also important to remember that, while I have for ease of writing referred in this book to the person who follows up with the newcomers as "minister," it can in fact be anyone. I started off by following up unofficially with newcomers as a layperson, *not even a lay leader*. Wise churches will train not only the minister but several of their friendliest, most knowledgeable people to greet newcomers, collect contact information, and follow up with newcomers. In small churches, it can easily fall to the minister alone, but it certainly doesn't have to.

"BUT WHAT IF DURING THE COFFEE MEETING A NEWCOMER DROPS A BOMB ON A LAY LEADER OR ASKS THEM A BIBLE QUESTION THEY DON'T KNOW THE ANSWER TO?!"

This is a really great question because it is a real possibility. If this happens, don't panic. You are not the minister. If they ask you a question about the Bible or dogma or church history that you don't know the answer to, be honest and refer them to the minister. "That's a great question, and I really wish I knew!" is a great response. Tell them, "If it's all right with you, I'd like to pass this question to the minister because I know s/he will want to follow up with you. How would you feel about that?" If they drop a bomb on you—a deeply personal revelation or a question that is clearly indicative of something much bigger, listen as best you can. Acknowledge the impact that this has, and thank them for telling you. Tell them, "I know this is something that the minister will want to help you with. How would you feel about me letting her/him know your concern and asking him to call you today or tomorrow?" Oftentimes if they have a concern of this nature, they will simply say, "Well, there is something else I want to ask, but I kind of want to talk to the minister about it." Reassure them and pass along the minister's contact information and a realistic timeline for a response.

"WHAT ABOUT PROBLEM PARISHIONERS? WHAT ABOUT PEOPLE WHO APPROACH NEWCOMERS WITH A BUNCH OF UNCOMFORTABLE TOUCHY-FEELIES? WHAT IF THEY CONVEY A FEELING OF DESPERATION?"

Invariably there is at least one church in every workshop that asks me some variation of this question. Often churches ask me to come train them on-site because they have this problem and want me to counsel them on how to deal with it.

In one case that I consulted with, the church was near a university, so they got a steady trickle of college students. The church was in decline. One well-meaning but misguided member would approach every college student that came in with a fierce handshake, and with a fiery and reverent look in her eyes say, "The moment you walked in I felt the Holy Spirit move and I knew that God had just sent us our new youth director!" They were devastated that none of these young people ever returned and had to figure out how to redirect this enthusiastic but somewhat inhibiting member. More often, church members simply say innocent but detrimental comments like, "It's great to see a new face!" or "Since I see you are a visitor, I have a special bag of goodies for you," or jump into, "How did you hear about us?" that identifies the person as an unknown anomaly before taking the polite step of allowing the visitor to identify themselves.

Some churches complain of the well-meaning, harmless, but nonconsensual hugger. In one church we were role-playing asking the newcomer for their contact information. The lay leader shook the "newcomer's" hand and then didn't let go for the rest of the conversation. The entire time he talked to the "newcomer," his free hand gently stroked their back and shoulder.

There was once a woman who was the oldest in the church and who had been there longer than any other person. Now age 83, she had begun attending when she was in college. She was dismayed—angry even—that her church was declining and figured that as unofficial matriarch she would have to single-handedly take the church back to its golden era. She would greet newcomers quickly and aggressively in order to show the minister that she could do his job better than him. If the minister followed up with someone and they came back, she would find something to criticize so that they wouldn't further take the church in the wrong direction.

Unfortunately, it is often the folks with the poorest boundaries who fancy themselves the church's most indispensable greeters. In these cases, a frank conversation is needed. Explain to the person that you are trying new strategies for greeting newcomers and you are finding that touching a person you don't know well—beyond a brief handshake—is always inappropriate. Ask them to please stop. The same goes for desperate exclamations such as asking them to be the new Youth Director. Explain to them that in this new strategy you follow a simple formula, and you have learned that even though they have been doing this for years and may think it is helpful, it may in fact be causing damage. Again, ask them to please stop and invite them to learn the new method. Healthy people who want the best for the church will be grateful you told them and ask to learn more so that they can work with the team and do better.

In workshops we role-play extensively so that everyone can practice being a greeter, everyone can feel what it is like to be a newcomer, and everyone watches the role-play so that everyone has a chance to give and receive feedback. In my experience, if in a workshop we see twenty different pairs get up to practice this, the first one is always the choppiest. The second one is markedly better. The third is pretty darn good. After that they run relatively smoothly. That is because practice makes perfect, but most importantly, because having instant feedback helps people to be aware of and improve upon habits they didn't even realize they had. Watching other people mess up increases our own awareness. Sometimes that is all it takes. Again, while people may in general feel that this is the minister's job, I always encourage churches to send a team of five people to learn how to do this. When I pair people up, I pair people from different churches so that they don't know each other when they are role-playing.

If you can find a team of five people to do this at your church, then take the time to practice. Have someone pretend to be a newcomer and take turns being the greeter. Do it in the sanctuary or at the entrance so you can get comfortable with the logistics. Hold this book open in front of you, if you need to, and simply read the script out loud. Then ask the other team members to tell you what you did well and what you could have improved on. They will tell you whether your stance is open or closed, whether you remembered to smile, stood too close, held the handshake too long, sounded sincere or rehearsed, went off script with a case of diarrhea of the mouth, or should have had your pen and newcomer card closer at hand. Most importantly, take turns being newcomers who refuse to give their contact information for any reason or none at all. This will give you an excellent opportunity to respond appropriately to rejection and lower the anxiety level in general.

There are some cases in which people cannot or will not maintain appropriate boundaries and there are many reasons for this. I will say right now that this usually falls along gender lines and more often than not it is males who have these issues. But not always. In many cases, it is due to older generation males who were simply raised with a very different understanding of how to interact with women. They honestly have the best of intentions, but cannot stop at a simple handshake. These are the bear-huggers, the hand-kissers, the back-strokers, the painful hand-shakers that simply don't let go, the ones who lean in so far that they are inches from the woman's face. Oftentimes they are simply hard of hearing (and for those hard of hearing it is often women's voices that are the hardest to hear).

Sometimes it is with much more deliberate mal-intent. I had a church complain to me of a married man who without fail hit on every female newcomer that came in the doors, often before greeters could even get there. I have had groups of church women take me aside and warn me about the man who always feinted a handshake but then smothered their hands with wet, sloppy kisses or snuck up on them from behind and surprised them with back-rubs. There was once a lay leader who would greet female visitors by sitting next to them in the pews and placing a hand on their knee while introducing himself.

In these cases, churches will often tell me one of two things. Either everyone in the church is afraid to have the conversation with the gentleman, or they will say they've tried to talk to him about it for years and there has been either no change or an angry response. In fact, when the greeter mentioned earlier held the handshake and stroked the "newcomer's" back for the entire conversation, even though the "newcomer" was visibly uncomfortable, no one in the group mentioned it when giving feedback. Even the man role-playing the "newcomer" said nothing at all about it. Instead, there was nervous laughter while everyone told him what a great job he did. When I diplomatically pointed out what he had done and reiterated that we never put our hands on newcomers except for a brief handshake, he withdrew angrily and refused to participate any more. He sat in a chair in the corner of the room and watched the rest of the workshop with a scowl on his face. The entire interaction from start to finish was telling of the climate in the church. They had reached a point where they rarely even saw newcomers anymore, and it was no mystery why. I told him privately and the rest of the group together that he was not the best person to be greeting people. I don't know whether they heeded my advice, and without more professional help they may not have been able to.

In these cases, it is not an individual problem, but a systemic problem. In this case, the church has a system which allows this individual's behavior to continue unabated, and that is why it does. They are more afraid of this individual's negative reaction than they are of losing first-time visitors or even sexual harassment lawsuits. If this is the case, then the entire system must be treated and the entire congregation may need to do some serious work around boundary training, male-female dynamics, and appropriate responses to inappropriate behavior. In our area there is an ordained minister who specializes in helping churches deal with situations of this sort. If your church has an individual that demonstrates inappropriate boundaries, and people are generally uncomfortable but afraid to say anything, get help from outside the church immediately.

"WHOSE JOB IS IT, REALLY?"

It's everybody's job. The entire congregation should able to greet a newcomer and ask them whether they've had a chance to fill out a visitor card with their contact information.

"BUT THEN WON'T THE NEWCOMER BE OVERWHELMED BY PEOPLE ASKING THEM FOR THEIR CONTACT INFORMATION?"

No, because the congregation will be cognizant. If they see the newcomer talking with a greeter and one of them writing some-thing down, they can draw reasonable conclusions and simply approach to say hello. People on the greeter team will be able to do a quick check-in in the moment—"Did you see that couple come in? Did you see anyone approach them already?" "Yeah, Gwen talked to them already. Let's go say hello." A very simple, "Are those four together?" "No, that's one family and that guy is by himself. I'll go talk to the guy if you want to talk to the family. Do you have your pen and visitor card?" It will only take a second and after a few weeks of practice it will happen very naturally. If you ask a newcomer whether they've had a chance to fill out a visitor card and they already have, then say, "Great!" and ask a get-to-know-you question. They won't be overwhelmed—they'll be pleased that the congregation is so friendly.

"I GAVE THIS SCRIPT TO MY WELCOME TEAM AND GREETERS AND THEY WON'T USE IT RIGHT AND THEY HATE IT AND IT'S NOT WORKING."

I often get emails from folks who read my blog articles or took my workshop, and loved the idea so much that they gave the script to their ushers and told them to start using it with all first-time visitors immediately. This often causes problems right off the bat. The greeters, having no understanding of the theory, statistics, or reason behind the change, will not jive with the script. Without having done any of the personal work to identify their fears or practice, they will get a case of the jitters. Having no context for the text of the actual script, they will say something off-the-cuff, like, "Can I get your phone number so we can follow up with you sometime this week?" Someone will think this sounds way too aggressive. This will be reported to the church busybody. With one failure hot off the presses, this entire new system will be called into question. Complaint letters will be sent to the minister. The minister will push back. The greeters will revolt. People will start talking about bringing back the pew pads so that no one will be perceived as "pushy."

I'd like you to take a moment to reflect on how much work we had to go through before we were able to embrace a new system. It wasn't as simple as just getting a new script in hand. If it were that simple, then I would never have had to turn this into an all-day workshop where two-thirds of the day is spent processing fear. It would never have become a full-length book. While it is true that there may be a rare bird out there who is absolutely fearless and can use a new script flawlessly with nary so much as a warm-up or explanation, most of the rest of the world needs a little more lead-in.

I would caution you against asking anyone to just use this new system without taking the time to walk them through the process that you have just gone through. A great way to start would be to ask them all to read this book, and then the ones that feel most enthusiastic about trying this system as it is presented should be the basis of your new greeting team. In general, churches do not respond well to having new systems forced on them. If people are pushed to use a new system with no training, they will either change it to make it feel less threatening or revolt altogether. It would be much, much better for you to take the bull by the horns personally and do it yourself every time. When you start having successes, people will start to approach you about the new system you are using. Those that seem most enthusiastic would be good candidates to start a conversation with, after which you can then give them a copy of this book.

A NEW VISION, A NEW REALITY

I want you to take a moment now to imagine yourself in your sanctuary. Very much like our earlier visioning exercise, it is on a Sunday morning. The choir is warming up, the choir director is playing the piano, and there is the general hustle and bustle of people lighting candles, placing flowers, and setting out the communion elements. People are coming in and finding seats. In the midst of all this, you see a person enter the sanctuary whom you don't recognize. They are clearly a first-time visitor. You recognize that it took a lot for them to pull themselves together emotionally and physically, get up early, and come to church today. You can tell they're a little nervous; there is a lot of sensory overload going on. You have no idea how many churches they have visited—and never returned to—before they came to yours. You can see that they are glancing around looking for a place to sit, some direction as to what to do, a friendly face. You're guessing they have some baggage they are bringing in from previous church or life experiences, and yet they are still here. They are seeking spiritual depth and integrity, a place to grow their faith and ask big questions. They are seeking a place where they can use their gifts and greatest joys to make a lasting difference in their societies. They are looking for a place where they can truly be themselves, even though they are not perfect. They are looking for a place that cares.

You recognize that you are being presented with an incredible opportunity to be a true reflection of God's love and God's light and God's radical welcome for them. You get to be a friendly face in a sea of strangers. You have the incredible opportunity to be that first friend they make, the one that is going to make a real difference in whether they come back and get involved. You get to show them that all of their efforts have not gone to waste, and have not gone unnoticed. So you take a big breath, walk up to them with a smile, shake their hand and welcome them, and then tell them how you'd like to take them for a cup of coffee so you can get to know them better and answer any questions they may have. When they say they'd like that, you ask them for their contact information.

Take a moment to imagine this scenario. Let it sit with you for a few moments. When you know where you feel it in your body, put your hand on that place.

If you are like most of the people who have taken my workshops, your hand is resting on your heart. You can feel a warmth and a comfort and a deep sense of love that you want to share with this new person. You may feel a little nervous, but mostly you feel peace and enthusiasm. There may even be a smile on your face.

You are ready.

THE GREAT COMMISSION AND THE FIVE GREAT FAILURES

ere's what I have learned after teaching this for many years. The first time I ever taught this workshop, it was at the annual gathering for our conference. The room was filled and there were at least sixty ministers and lay leaders in attendance. I collected contact information from every single one of them and followed up a week later to ask them two questions:

1. Did you use what you learned last Sunday?
2. Did it work?

Two of the attendees said, "Yes! We had three first-time visitors last week and I approached all of them and got contact information. They all said yes to coffee and they all came back this Sunday. It totally worked!" These churches have since tracked their numbers and more than 80% of their visitors return and many of them stay and become part of the congregation. Their churches are steadily growing.

The rest said something like this:

"Oh my goodness, I *loved* your workshop. It had such good information! So on Sunday I went right up to my minister and told him all about it. He thought it sounded like a great idea so he encouraged me to go to the church moderator. So the moderator said that they can put it on the church agenda when they meet in three months. I'm totally going to try and get the church to put together a committee that can work out a rotating schedule of official contact information gatherers. Then we can get them trained and ..." and six months later nothing had been done, and the one to two visitors per week quietly came and left again and never returned.

After reading this book, it will be very tempting to send this to committee. You may have a very strong urge to go to your councils and your boards and try to form a committee or a team, to make it official. You may think you need to ask permission, you may think you need to make a rotating schedule. You may spend a lot of time thinking about whose job this should be and how to get them to do it.

The reality is, it is your job. Jesus never said, "Convene the church council at a regularly scheduled meeting and make sure that after making this an agenda item they vote to assign the role of greeter/newcomer follow-up to the minister..."

Jesus said, "Go therefore and make disciples of all nations..." (Matthew 28:19).

"And if you greet only your brothers and sisters, what more are you doing than others? Do not even the Gentiles do the same? Be perfect, therefore, as your heavenly Father is perfect" (Matthew 5:47-48).

The book of Romans reiterates: "Welcome one another, therefore, just as Christ has welcomed you, for the glory of God" (Romans 15:7).

Some people really honestly do believe that they must have permission before they can do this work in their church. I didn't ask permission before I started schlepping the guestbook around twenty years ago. What you are doing requires no money, so you don't need to go to the council to ask for a line item on the budget. What you are doing requires no church resources, so you don't need to ask anyone's permission to rent a room or order supplies. It does not require an announcement in the church newsletter or in the bulletin. All it requires is your willing spirit and a pen that you can bring from home.

You do not need to organize a team, though you may find that as you use this method, curious parishioners may ask what you are doing and even be inspired to help.

You may want to check in with the minister if you are going to be helping them to collect the contact information, but they will be the one to follow up. Other than that, you don't need permission.

But if permission is what you are waiting for, then I give you permission. I bless you and commission you to follow Jesus' commandment to greet one another and make disciples of all nations. You have within you right this very moment all of the skills, resources, gifts, and information that you need to be able to walk up to the next first-time visitor you see and greet them, ask them for their contact information, and follow up with them. If you wait until you have someone's permission, council approval, and an organized rotating system, you'll never do it. So don't wait.

Just try it. And give yourselves permission to fail. An old professor of mine once gave our class sage advice which I have heeded many times. Every church gets five great failures. FIVE. Every time a church tries something new, it gets to fall flat on its face five times before it really catches on and runs smoothly. So give yourself five great failures. Over the next several weeks or months, you will approach newcomers and flub it up. You will say the wrong thing. You will get nervous and talk too fast. You will forget your pen and visitor card. You will try to leave a message on their answering machine and make an embarrassing mistake. It will happen. Let it go. The first five are par for the course, and God will send you more chances to practice your skills in a week or so. It will get easier. It will get smoother. You will soon have more successes than failures, and then you will really think it's fun. When it starts to bear fruit, when more and more people stay and the pews start to fill up and more and more people start to join, you will realize that all your apprehension was for naught. You will wonder why you ever hesitated in the first place. So go. Just dive in.

Go with many blessings. If it works, please email me and tell me! I want to know! If something goes terribly wrong, email me too. I'll help you figure it out.

Many Blessings,

Rev. Tracy Barnowe
pastortracy@howtogrowmychurch.com
www.howtogrowmychurch.com